Innovative Practices for Teaching Sign Language Interpreters

CYNTHIA B. ROY, *Editor*

Innovative Practices
for Teaching
Sign Language Interpreters

GALLAUDET UNIVERSITY PRESS
Washington, D.C.

Gallaudet University Press
Washington, DC 20002

Library of Congress Cataloging-in-Publication Data

Innovative practices for teaching sign language interpreters / Cynthia B. Roy, editor.
   p. cm.
   Includes bibliographical references and index.
   ISBN 1-56368-088-2
   1. Interpreters for the deaf—Training of—United States. 2. Sign language—
Study and teaching—United States. 3. American Sign Language—Study and
teaching. I. Roy, Cynthia B., 1950–

HV2402.I56   2000
419—dc21   99-059244

CONTENTS

Contributors vii

Foreword ix
 ROBERT INGRAM

Training Interpreters—Past, Present, and Future 1
 CYNTHIA B. ROY

Discourse Mapping: Developing Textual Coherence
Skills in Interpreters 15
 ELIZABETH A. WINSTON AND
 CHRISTINE MONIKOWSKI

Critical Linguistic and Cultural Awareness:
Essential Tools in the Interpreter's Kit Bag 67
 KYRA POLLITT

Interactive Role-Plays As a Teaching Strategy 83
 MELANIE METZGER

Translation Techniques in Interpreter Education 109
 JEFFREY E. DAVIS

Metacognition and Recall Protocols in
the Interpreting Classroom   132
RICO PETERSON

Portfolios: One Answer to the Challenge of
Assessment and the "Readiness to Work" Gap   153
JANICE H. HUMPHREY

Index   177

CONTRIBUTORS

Jeffrey E. Davis, Ph.D.
Interpreter Education Program
Miami-Dade Community College
Miami, Florida

Janice H. Humphrey, Ed.D.
Program of Sign Language
Interpretation
Douglas College
New Westminster, British
Columbia, Canada

Robert Ingram
Program Manager
California Relay Service
Riverbank, California

Melanie Metzger, Ph.D.
Department of ASL, Linguistics,
and Interpretation
Gallaudet University
Washington, D.C.

Christine Monikowski, Ph.D.
Department of ASL and
Interpreting Education
National Technical Institute of
the Deaf
Rochester Institute of Technology
Rochester, New York

Rico Peterson, Ph.D.
Department of ASL and
Interpreting Education
National Technical Institute
for the Deaf
Rochester Institute of
Technology
Rochester, New York

Kyra Pollitt, M.A., RSLI
Sign Languages International
(UK base)
Huddlestone's Wharf
Newark, England

Cynthia B. Roy, Ph.D.
ASL/English Interpreting
Program
Department of English
Indiana University/Purdue
University Indianapolis
Indianapolis, Indiana

Elizabeth A. Winston, Ph.D.
Educational Linguistics
Research Center
Loveland, Colorado

ROBERT INGRAM

FOREWORD

IN 1972 THE Registry of Interpreters for the Deaf (RID) and Gallaudet College (it wasn't a university yet) convened the Conference on Preparation of Personnel in the Field of Interpreting. The idea was to bring together experts who could suggest what skills and knowledge would-be interpreters needed to have and how best to develop those skills and that knowledge. Most of the "experts" present came from the fields of deaf education and rehabilitation. There were only one or two psychologists, no anthropologists, no sociologists, no interculturalists, no linguists, and no teachers of translation or interpretation of spoken languages.

William Stokoe, the first linguist to study ASL (and still one of the very few at that time), had been invited but was unable to attend. I attended, not as an "expert," but as the recorder and editor of the conference proceedings. I had graduated from the University of Southern Mississippi only a few months before with a bachelor's degree in communication and only a minor in linguistics, but that was enough to establish me as the resident linguist at the table.

The conference participants produced a list of skills and knowledge that an interpreter would need, but most of the items on the list had more to do with the clarity of signing and fingerspelling and the role of the interpreter than with the processing of linguistic information in a cross-cultural context. The nature of meaning and the understanding of discourse were not discussed at all. The papers in this volume stand in sharp contrast to the prevailing view of interpreter training in 1972. They bring discourse, culture, and context center stage.

WHY DISCOURSE MATTERS

As I write these words, I am thinking that I should now offer the reader a weighted opinion as to *why* an understanding of discourse matters in interpreter training. Rather than offer a philosophical explanation, though, I will follow the lead of my co-authors and give an example from my own teaching experience. This activity (or set of activities) is based on Kathleen Callow's little-known, but very significant book, *Discourse Considerations in Translating the Word of God* (1974).

Callow posits that "different types of speech are appropriate in different situations." She describes the six major types of discourse as follows:

1. Narrative—"recounts a series of events ordered more or less chronologically";
2. Procedural—"give(s) instructions as to the accomplishing of a task or achieving of an object";
3. Hortatory—which we might also call persuasive discourse, "attempts to influence conduct";
4. Explanatory—"seeks to provide information required in particular circumstances";
5. Argumentative—"attempts to prove something to the hearer";
6. Conversational—is a conversation between two or more people (1974, 13).

Discourse types do not always stand alone. Conversational discourse, for example, may contain elements of narrative, procedural, and explanatory discourse. In some languages, narrative and descriptive discourse may constitute a single type, or hortatory and procedural discourse may be found to overlap significantly.

The beauty of Callow's work is not in the categorizing of the six types of discourse, however, but in the demonstration of the fact that certain linguistic forms are more likely to occur with some discourse types than with others. For example, narrative discourse and procedural discourse are both likely to proceed according to chronological order, but that chronology is more likely to be in the past tense with narrative discourse and in future or habitual present tense with procedural discourse. Explanatory discourse often accomplishes its objective by "providing detailed descriptions of a person, situation or activity," while argumentative discourse "tends to exhibit frequent contrast between two opposing themes" (1974, 13). Callow also found that person orientation, sentence length, and the involvement of the narrator and the person addressed can differentiate one discourse type from another.

During the spring semester of 1997, I taught a course in consecutive interpretation at Ohlone College. To prepare for this course I reviewed Callow's work and became convinced that her insights would be useful in teaching students more effectively to become good interpreters. Here is what I did: I began by having the students read the first chapter of Callow's book and discuss the linguistic and discourse structures associated with each of the six discourse types. At the next class session, I wrote the following speech title on the board: "Backpacking in Yosemite." I instructed the students to imagine that they would be interpreting this speech and to describe what they thought it would be like in each of the six discourse types (i.e., narrative, procedural, hortatory, explanatory, argumentative, and conversational). Through this activity, students began to understand that the differences in discourse types are real, not just theoretical, and that knowledge of these differences might aid them in their interpreting tasks.

But the activity was not finished. I then passed around a sheet of paper containing the following six speech titles:

1. The Making of Silicon Chips
2. The Making of a Champion
3. Values versus Behavior in Implementing Organizational Change in a Non-Union Corporation
4. The Day the Music Died
5. Why You Should Invest in No-Load Mutual Funds
6. An Interview with Stephen Hawking

"Judging from the title of the speech alone," I asked the students, "what type of discourse would you expect each of these speeches to

represent: narrative, procedural, hortatory, explanatory, argumentative, or conversational?" Of course, there were no right or wrong
answers, and, in fact, there might be more than one good answer for
any given title, but from this activity students learned to anticipate
discourse types and (later) grammatical patterns most likely to occur
with those discourse types based on nothing more than a title. They
also learned from their discussion that a title can be misleading at
first glance and that sometimes additional information is needed before an interpreter can accurately assess what type of discourse a
speech really is. Finally, they learned to recognize certain words or
phrases as clues to the type of discourse that was to follow. For example, the words "why" and "reason" often signal hortatory discourse; "how to" and "steps" often indicate procedural discourse;
"versus," "or," and "comparison" often mean that argumentative
discourse is just ahead; "story" and "tale" are often associated with
narrative discourse; and "description" often suggests explanatory
discourse.

For the remainder of the course, before students would interpret
a corpus in either English or ASL, I would give them the title, and
we would discuss what type of discourse it was likely to be. After the
exercise, we would talk about whether or not our predictions were
correct and what we actually observed. Students were also tested on
this ability in both midterm and final exams.

More important than simply identifying discourse types, however, was learning to associate certain grammatical structures with
specific types of discourse. Table 1 shows some of the linguistic or
discourse features that we often found with each type of discourse.

What this example—and the others described in this volume—
illustrates is that an understanding of the relationship between theory and application is not just valuable to teachers of interpretation;
it is indispensable. Cynthia Roy has been a pioneer in this crusade
for more years than either of us would probably care to count. With
this volume, she not only breaks new ground, but shows us where we
must go if we are to succeed in meeting the demand for qualified interpreters in the future. I can think of no one more qualified to lead
the way.

Table 1. Grammatical Features Associated with Specific Discourse Types

Features	Discourse Types					
	Narrative	Procedural	Explanatory	Argumentative	Hortatory	Conversational
Ordering						
Logical				X	X	
Chronological	X	X				
Nonlinear, random			X			X
Flashbacks	X					X
Rate & Pausing						
Fast, pauses for effect	X					
Slower, pauses between components		X	X			
Slower, pauses for comprehension & response		X	X	X	X	
Variable, pauses for effect or turn-taking						X
Tense						
Present or future		X				
Past	X					
Use of Space						
Set up scenes & characters	X					
Set up objects or categories		X	X			
Set up ideas				X	X	

continued on next page

Table 1. Grammatical Features Associated with Specific Discourse Types (*continued*)

Features	Narrative	Procedural	Explanatory	Argumentative	Hortatory	Conversational
Numbering						
Sequential		X				
Rank-ordered					X	
Voice & Mood						
Lots of passive voice			X			
Commands		X				
Action verbs	X	X				
Stative verbs ("be")			X		X	
Point of View						
Objective (facts)	X	X	X			
Subjective (opinions)				X	X	
Register						
Formal					X	
Consultative		X				
Casual	X					X

Level						
Abstract		X				X
Concrete	X				X	
Other Characteristics						
Personification	X					
Role taking & body shifting	X					X
Proper nouns	X					
Descriptive adjectives/adverbs			X			
Incomplete sentences						X
Classifiers	X			X		
Rhetorical questions				X	X	X
Technical terminology				X		
Quotations	X					X

BACK TO THE FUTURE

As I look over these papers and look back to the Conference on the Preparation of Personnel in the Field of Interpreting held in 1972, I can't help but wonder if it isn't time for the new pioneers to convene a new conference, one that brings together not only innovators in the field, but also experts from outside of the field—cognitive psychologists, neuroscientists, engineers, statisticians, logicians, anthropologists, interculturalists, computer scientists, semioticians, linguists of various types, and others who might bring fresh and radically creative perspectives to the question of what exactly this thing that we call interpreting really is and how we might best teach people how to do it. I would expect to see all the contributors in this volume present at such a conference.

REFERENCES

Callow, K. 1974. *Discourse considerations in translating the word of God.* Grand Rapids, Mich.: Zondervan.
Ingram, R., ed. 1972. *Conference on the preparation of personnel in the field of interpreting.* Washington, D.C.: Gallaudet University.

Innovative Practices for Teaching Sign Language Interpreters

CYNTHIA B. ROY

Training Interpreters—
Past, Present, and Future

EVER SINCE the formal education of interpreters began, educators
have been trying to determine what to teach in order to produce
entry-level interpreters who achieve the minimum level of competence needed to perform their jobs successfully. Etilvia Arjona, former director of the translation and interpretation program at the
Monterey Institute of International Studies, suggested that interpreter training programs should take students to levels in which they
"routinely transfer or interpret the message accurately and appropriately, thus bridging the communicative gap in a meaningful manner" (1983, 6). The notion that beginning interpreters should be
able to consistently convey accurate and appropriate messages—no
matter what the situation or event—is intriguing. Nevertheless, this
concept is consistent with the way that other professions construct
their educational programs. How best to teach students a body of
knowledge, as well as a professional skill, that adequately meets
entry-level requirements is a question most interpreter-training
programs are still trying to answer.

One problem is a profession-wide lack of agreement about
what constitutes a basic, or generic, interpreted meeting and what
an interpreter must know and be able to do to participate in an appropriate way. Training programs typically base courses and curricula on theories borrowed from translation studies, spoken-language
training exercises, and information-processing techniques. They
also practice interpreting as it is done in specialized settings such
as schools, doctors' offices, and courtrooms. Interpreting courses,
consciously or unconsciously, are designed around the concept of an

1

interpreter as a producer of a *text*—a singular, bounded entity of words, sentences, or signs. In such a framework, the correctness (or equivalence) of the text is central, speakers are secondary, and listeners are typically anonymous. Interpreters are—and students learn to think of themselves as—passive conveyors of others' words and thoughts. Most programs accept this set of beliefs about an interpreter's role and pay little, if any, attention to the nature of interpreted situations or to the other participants within such situations.

When educators do have a chance to gather and discuss training, they rarely discuss fundamental notions such as those just considered. Rather, they present teaching activities at conferences, which permit only a brief exchange of ideas or activities. Extended discussion, practice, and evaluation are precluded by time constraints. These activities are often presented as random teaching strategies, without grounding in theoretical notions of language, or in interaction among people, or in connections to research. Instructors who take home "new" ideas are often unable to determine their place in a curriculum, and they do not have a sequential, scaffolding learning structure that allows them to incorporate the "new" activity and then proceed to the next stage. Courses thus become haphazard strings of exercises and activities that lack a clear purpose.

However, when educators have advanced training in language study, such as linguistics, and are also researchers, formulating studies to answer questions about learning, their teaching expertise combines with acquired knowledge. They grow professionally as teachers and report that their teaching improves with a new awareness of why students learn the way they do. When successful teachers—those who base their teaching strategies on theory and research—are invited to demonstrate and discuss their own best practices, the profession benefits from their insight and expertise.

An educational reform movement already in practice in the United States—the National Writing Project—elicits the best techniques of classroom teachers and asks them to connect their practice to theory and research. This successful professional development model can also work for teachers of interpreters. Thus the contributors in this book each share a teaching practice that they consider particularly effective with their students.

A Brief Overview of ASL/English Interpreter Training

The first collegiate sign language interpreter-training programs were established in the mid-1970s and were located in speech communication or deaf education programs in universities or community colleges. Most programs started with one or two interpreter training classes, usually taught by individuals who were experienced interpreters but who had little or no advanced academic training in related fields. The curricula of such programs developed gradually. Most started by teaching sign language, whether American Sign Language (ASL) or contact signing. After a year or more, students were deemed ready to begin interpreter training regardless of their general level of education, their abilities in English, or their exposure to Deaf adults or children.

As these programs developed, linguistic discoveries defining American Sign Language as a language with the same descriptive and structural levels as spoken languages emerged. During the 1970s and 1980s, linguists described grammatical structure in ASL that was so new and interesting that it became the main focus of teaching interpreting. Now that ASL and English were defined as two *languages* across which interpreters worked, educators began to look at spoken-language interpreter training and noted that in those programs students had to possess a high degree of fluency in *both* languages as well as a broad, liberal-arts background. At interpreting conferences and in newsletters, educators began to call not only for greater fluency in ASL but also a fluency indicative of heightened mastery in spoken English (McIntire 1980; Yoken 1979). At that time, the only way to raise the level of mastery or fluency in both languages and to obtain a liberal arts background was through university bachelor-degree programs.

However, many programs remained at the community-college level. Because community colleges have open-admission policies, fluency in either ASL or English could neither be required nor achieved in two years. Universities also allowed students who had no fluency in ASL to enter interpreting programs but then had to focus a great deal of attention on teaching ASL. In many such programs, beginning interpreting classes were actually advanced ASL classes. That meant, practically speaking, that the interpreter-training segment was really a program of increasing fluency. Bringing students to adequate levels of fluency consumed so much program time that few instructors had to consider what they would teach a student who was fluent in ASL and had an adequate command of English. In addition, the texts used for interpreting practice focused on storytelling rather than the type of talk interpreting consumers would use in a doctor's or a social security office.

When students eventually moved into interpreting classes and attempted interpreting to and from English, vocabulary and sentences were the focus—they learned which signs were "conceptually accurate" for specific English words, phrases, and sentences. Decisions about meaning focused on the word level and the production of an interpreted message that accurately mirrored the source message. Although easier for students with little training in linguistics (Baker 1992, 6), this approach—taking words and phrases as starting points for defining units of meaning—is not in line with current understanding of the nature of discourse, meaning, and interaction between communicants (Goffman 1981, Gumperz 1982, Wadensjö 1998). In fact, it contributes to the faulty notion that words (or signs) in and of themselves have meanings that do not change over the course of an interpretation and can be transformed with only a dictionary knowledge of a language. Although words have meanings as they stand alone in a dictionary-type, static sense, they begin to acquire multiple, layered meanings the minute they are exchanged, connected to experiences, and used by people within specific situations and times.

When interpreting skills were taught specifically, instructors employed a methodology of successive approximation, according to which students were provided with texts, either spoken English or ASL, and were expected to produce simultaneous interpretation from the outset of their training (rather than acquiring this complex skill in stages). The goal of this sort of training was to gradually improve the degree to which a student's target language product approximated a quality interpretation.

Although many of the instructors were community interpreters, the bulk of whose interpreting consisted of interaction among three participants, courses were structured as though conference (or platform) interpreting were the typical model of interpreting. When interpreting for a single speaker, the focus is on the informational content of a message. Thus courses came to emphasize primarily details of the message's surface form rather than the communicative situation as a whole. Accordingly, teaching then focused on accuracy and speed.

Cognitive psychologists and psycholinguists, whose central area of interest was language processing and transference, conducted much of the early research on interpreting. Focusing on the complexity of the tasks of simultaneously listening, understanding, reformulating, and speaking, this research produced detailed models of the cognitive stages necessary to perform the task of interpreting (Gerver 1976; Moser 1978; Cokely 1984). Research into cognitive processes involved hypothesizing about what went on in the minds of interpreters, which often resulted in the application of deductive, experimental, or quasi-experimental research. The logic behind such studies concentrates on omissions and distortions, asking questions such as What gets lost? and What gets added? Studies with this orientation thus prescribed what interpreters *ought* to be doing and saying. Success or failure was defined as the degree to which the interpreted message approximated the source message rather than whether the participants perceived the event as successful and whether the task of a meeting was accomplished.

This perspective misses the complex ways in which talk is dynamic, going back and forth between two or more speakers while they ask questions, argue, complain, or joke. Also missed is the dynamic activity during which the interpreter assists this exchange and manages the direction and flow of talk. Imagined listeners—and their responses and expectations—are not considered or assigned any importance. Talk as text is removed from the natural process of ordinary conversation and conversational features such as two speakers talking at the same time, one speaker correcting a misunderstanding, or one speaker talking directly to an interpreter.

Elsewhere I have attributed this way of thinking to everyday perceptions about language and communication (Roy 1989, 1993) and to what Reddy (1979) calls the *conduit model* of language and communication. These conduit metaphors, used to describe the role and function of an interpreter, reveal an underlying perception of the interpreter's role as passive and neutral. These metaphors blind researchers and educators to a concept of the interpreter as a conversational participant who has an impact on a situation and almost obscure the impact individual speakers have on the situation.

Arjona was one of the first educators to base a program on the notion that "the translation [or interpreting] process is considered as taking place within a situational/cultural context that is, in itself, an integral part of the process and that must be considered in order to bridge, in a meaningful manner, the gap that separates both sender and receptor audiences. This transfer must encompass the unique linguistic, paralinguistic, and logic systems for interpersonal communication of both sender and receptor audiences" (1978, 36). Hers was the first program to consider the basic problems of communication, understanding, misunderstanding, and nonunderstanding. At the 1982 Conference of Interpreter Trainers (CIT), Arjona urged a task analysis of the interpreter's performance in order to build a curriculum that taught the task in a sequential and developmental order. At the next CIT conference, a task analysis was distributed, and attendees contributed to a lengthy list of various cognitive and personal tasks required to interpret (McIntire 1984). The major components were based on cognitive processes for which spoken language interpreter-training programs had developed exercises. Although programs were influenced to begin using some of these teaching strategies, such as shadowing, paraphrasing, dual-tasking, and ways to increase lag time, these strategies emerged from programs that trained conference interpreters and thus reemphasized a textual view of a speaker's production and the interpreted rendition.

As the decade progressed, educators turned to issues of power and identity, issues of teamwork, and specific interpreting types, such as educational and legal interpreting. In an age when the rights of minorities and issues of language oppression were of central concern, the bilingual, bicultural label came into widespread use. The problem with such a label, however, is that it never dispels the assumed model of interpreting and continues to focus on two independent, yet related, texts. This persistent model of a single speaker and an interpreter who conveys the content message has several inherent problems:

1. The focus is on the relaying of the message as the sole purpose of the interpreter and the participant who produces the message;
2. Talk as a way of doing something (such as informing, explaining, or complaining) is overlooked;
3. This approach cannot account for other conversation-related activities that are not a part of either text.

Thus the bilingual, bicultural label did not take us away from a basic conceptual notion of interpreting as relaying text that can then be judged as correct, appropriate, and equivalent. For example, in a 1998 issue of *Views*, the Registry of Interpreters for the Deaf newsletter, Hoza (an interpreter educator) posed the dilemma of a doctor, during a medical examination, asking the interpreter a direct question that was not about the medical interview itself or the patient but rather a conversational query about how the interpreter had learned sign language. Hoza suggested that when an interpreter is asked such direct questions by a participant, the issue is an ethical one having to do with where an interpreter's loyalties lie. Although teachers would agree that interpreting students need to know how to resolve ethical dilemmas, the difficulty posed here is actually an ordinary conversational occurrence common in medical interviews even when no interpreter is present. In medical exams, when a patient is otherwise occupied (dressing or having a temperature taken), a doctor may turn to other people in the room and make "small talk." Common sense suggests that this occurs naturally, and research on interpreters in such settings suggests that, rather than a protracted relay between participants, a brief response from an interpreter actually minimizes the interpreter's participation in a

situation in which the focus should remain on the primary participants (Metzger 1995). Although Hoza's discussion noted the situa-
tional context in which the question was asked, the discussion that
followed in no way accounted for ways in which people participate
in medical interviews, nor did it query the intentions or expectations
of any of the speakers in this event. Rather, the focus was on the
question—the text—which demonstrates the underlying assumptions of interpreting as a textual problem without considering the
reciprocal nature of conversation, the purpose of asking questions,
and he expectations and performance of all the participants.

Neglected is the interactive nature of most interpreting situations
and the complex nature of meaning produced by human beings who
are purposely interacting. An approach that emphasizes discourse
and interaction understands that people use language to do things
and that language always occurs within specific situations that are
composed of linguistic, social, and interactive conventions as well as
conversational styles and attributes. In a discourse approach, for
example, the question "Can I help you?" does not have the same
meaning, and thus the same interpretation, when uttered by a re-
ceptionist, a secretary, and a bank vice-president. The meaning of
this relatively simple question clearly depends on several factors,
such as the status of the persons uttering the question, their reasons
for asking, and their expectations for a response.

A New Approach

Researchers increasingly realized that interpreting is an active process of communicating between two languages and cultures and that
theoretical frameworks of social interaction, sociolinguistics, and
discourse analysis are more appropriate for analyzing the task of interpreting. My own study (Roy 1989) demonstrated that an interpreter actively participated in an interpreted event and made several
decisions in regard to taking turns within a teacher-student exchange. Wadensjö (1992) demonstrated that interpreters are asked
direct questions, and they answer them, ask for clarification, and
participate in the process, while Metzger (1995) demonstrated that

when an interpreter responds briefly to a direct question, the interpreter's effect on the communication is minimal.

This perspective in research (and teaching) explores the social order of real-life interpreter-mediated conversations. It tries to detect
what people in these situations expect as the adequate (should we say
"correct?") way to act, given the immediate situation. It asks what
norms of language use are valid in a given conversational event and
what norms are valid for which persons and why. As Wadensjö suggests, "For instance, what communicative conventions are involved
when an interpreter, talking on behalf of another person, suddenly
switches from 'I' to an emphasized 'she'?" (1998, 5).

The starting point for this research is speech activities or, as Wadensjö (1998) suggests, speech genres, situated in their sociocultural
context. These concepts come from the work of sociolinguists such
as John Gumperz (1982), sociologist Erving Goffman (1981), language philosopher Mikhail Bakhtin (1986), and others. From these
theoretical explanations of the nature of conversational interaction,
recent interpreting research has begun to seek participants' perspectives, "trying to find out what meaning *they* attribute to particular words; how phrases and stretches of talk make sense to different
actors in situated events" (Wadensjö 1998, 7). This approach forces
the perspective of interpreting as "dynamic inter-activity" (Wadensjö 1998, 7). And this perspective asks how *all* the participants
are making sense of what they are talking about, of what they are doing with talk. Interactional analysis then analyzes the ways in which
participants use language and discourse strategies and how they use
both language and strategies differently. Within this analysis, words
and longer phrases are simply one part of the whole picture.

This perspective sees talk as an *activity* in which participants determine minute-by-minute the meaning of something that is said.
This means that speakers and interpreters process information at
several levels. At any one point in a conversation, participants rely
on schemata or interpretive frames (Bateson 1982; Gumperz 1982;
Tannen 1979) based on their experiences with similar situations as
well as grammatical and lexical knowledge. In doing this speakers (and interpreters) rely on their knowledge of both variation and

ritual in language to interpret the significance of conversational options. When people engage in interpreter-mediated interaction,
they see themselves as doing things, such as asking for information, explaining, making a request, arguing, and so on. As participants talk back and forth, the meaning they assign to various words
and phrases becomes something they compose together, and all participants work to make sense of the talk. Words and utterances have
meanings and functions within layers of context, layers that are particular to the individual situation and to generalizable, recurring
situa. :ons. What participants say and mean can be understood only
when considered as part of a reciprocal process among the individuals present.

Acknowledging that interpreting is a discourse process in which
interpreters are active participants who need to know about and
understand interactional behavior as well as explicit ways in which
languages and cultures use language changes our perception of what
interpreters do. That is, interpreters make intentional, informed
choices from a range of possibilities. This altered perspective on
how interpreters actually accomplish their task will bring about a
change in educational practice. It suggests that what is significant in
the process of learning to interpret is understanding the nature of
social situations, being conscious of discourse processes, and knowing and recognizing ways of using language. Because these processes
and an interpreter's role are ineluctably bound to language and patterns of discourse, discourse analysis offers not only a new research
framework and a more accurate perception of a basic interpreted
interaction but also a new understanding of the important aspects of
teaching interpreting.

THE STRUCTURE OF THIS BOOK

As many curriculum specialists have noted, curriculum involves
putting into practice a set of beliefs concerning how people learn,
what they should be learning, and the contexts that will support that
learning (Short and Burke 1991). The practices explained in this
book come from a set of beliefs about the nature of interpreting, the
sequence in which people learn to interpret, and what students

should learn. Students in these programs study interpreting as a sociocultural-linguistic process that cannot be separated from either the language or its speakers.

As interpreters, researchers, and educators, the contributors to this volume each share one teaching practice that works in their classroom and is supported by current knowledge, research, and theory about how one learns to interpret. Each of their practices assumes that students learn to interpret effectively and fluently by becoming consciously aware of and in control of language processes. These practices are distinguished by the fact that they are drawn from research on language, learning, and interpreting. Successful teaching practices work for a reason, and making the connection to that reason is the basis of curriculum development.

In chapter 2 Winston and Monikowski explain *discourse mapping*, an application of discourse analysis that provides students with analytical experience so that their interpretations are effective. These interpretations are accurate in content, socially appropriate, and linguistically accurate. Discourse mapping is a strategy that teaches students to develop a mental picture of the meaning of a message. By doing so, students can reconstruct a similar map to produce an interpretation and can see the relationships of context, form, and content. Mapping is similar to techniques in reading and writing instruction and is referred to as concept mapping, mind mapping, or idea mapping. Discourse mapping also helps instructors choose more appropriate texts for students by highlighting the structure of themes within a text and the approach of the speaker.

In chapter 3 Pollitt explains the use of critical discourse analysis (CDA), a type of discourse analysis widely used in Europe. CDA sees discourse as ways in which speakers use language to portray their identities and alliances to the various cultures to which they belong. Because speakers use discourse to do things, critical discourse analysis allows researchers to pick apart what speakers say and reveal some of the influences and beliefs that shape their lives and the way they use language.

Metzger, in chapter 4, describes how to implement quality, interactive role-plays so that students learn strategies for switching back and forth rapidly between languages, for managing features of interaction (such as overlap), and for making relevant contributions to the interaction (such as indicating the source of an utterance). Her chapter includes how to prepare for role-plays, how to implement them, and how to give effective feedback.

In chapter 5 Davis describes the translation skills that form the basis for teaching consecutive interpreting, after which students move into simultaneous interpreting. Teaching translation skills is useful in moving students beyond the lexical and phrasal level to deeper levels of semantics and pragmatics. These strategies help students understand not only the intended meaning of the source message but also the manner in which the listeners are likely to understand the message.

In chapter 6 Peterson describes the use of recall protocols as both an instructional technique and as a metric for student comprehension of ASL discourse. In many sign language interpreting programs, students need further language learning, especially in ASL. Recall protocols can be used to teach metacognitive skills as well as to assess comprehension. A sample recall is provided, together with sample scoring.

In chapter 7 Humphrey explains her program's use of graduation portfolios to indicate a student's mastery (or lack of mastery) of the program outcomes identified by the faculty. Students compile written and videotaped evidence to demonstrate their readiness to enter the field of ASL/English interpretation; the resulting portfolio is assessed by a team of three individuals: a faculty member, a professional interpreter, and a member of the Deaf community. The team evaluates the portfolio and then recommends the student for graduation or remediation.

IT IS our hope that interpreting instructors will implement the practices explained in this book and that they, in turn, will demonstrate and discuss their own best practices. The field of interpreter education will benefit from tapping that particular knowledge of how to teach interpreting that comes from both theory and practice. In this process we will gain strength and become less defensive and more open. Such an atmosphere of trust breeds honest dialogue and a breaking down of traditional barriers, and, as a result, teachers can work together as mutually respected colleagues.

REFERENCES

Arjona, E. 1978. Intercultural communication and the training of interpreters at the Monterey Institute of International Studies. In *Language interpretation and communication*, ed. D. Gerver and H. W. Sinaiko, 35–44. New York: Plenum Press.

———. 1983. Issues in the design of curricula for the professional education of translators and interpreters. In *New dialogues in interpreter education* (Proceedings of the Third National Conference of Interpreter Trainers), ed. M. McIntire, 1–16. Silver Spring, Md.: RID Publications.

Baker, M. 1992. *In other words—A coursebook on translation.* London/New York: Routledge.

Bakhtin, M. 1986. *Speech genres and other late essays.* Ed. C. Emerson and M. Holquist, trans. V. W. McGee. Austin: University of Texas Press.

Bateson, G. 1972. *Steps to an ecology of mind.* New York: Ballantine.

Frishberg, N. 1986. *Interpreting: An introduction.* Silver Spring, Md.: RID Publications.

Gerver, D. 1976. Empirical studies of simultaneous interpretation: A review and a model. In *Translation: Applications and research*, ed. R. Brislin. New York: Gardner Press.

Goffman, E. *Forms of talk.* Philadelphia: University of Pennsylvania Press.

Gumperz, J. 1982. *Discourse strategies.* Cambridge: Cambridge University Press.

Hoza, J. 1998. The loyalty question. *Views* 15(1): 6–7.

McIntire, M. 1980. Some linguistic factors in training sign to voice interpreters. In *A century of Deaf awareness in a decade of interpreting awareness* (Proceedings of the 1980 RID Convention), ed. F. Caccamise, 189–97. Silver Spring, Md.: RID Publications.

———, ed. 1984. Task analysis of interpretation and transliteration. In *New dimensions in interpreter education: Task analysis—Theory and application* (Proceedings of the Fifth National RID Convention). Silver Spring, Md.: RID Publications.

Metzger, M. 1995. The paradox of neutrality: A comparison of interpreters' goals with the realities of interactive discourse. Ph.D. diss., Georgetown University, Washington, D.C.

Moser, B. 1978. Simultaneous interpretation: A hypothetical model and its practical application. In *Language interpretation and communication*, ed. D. Gerver and H. W. Sinaiko, 353–68. New York: Plenum Press.

Reddy, M. 1993. The conduit metaphor: A case of frame conflict in our language about language. In *Metaphor and thought*, 2d ed., ed. A. Ortony, 164–201. Cambridge: Cambridge University Press.

Roy, C. 1989. A sociolinguistic analysis of the interpreter's role in the turn exchanges of an interpreted event. Ph.D. diss., Georgetown University, Washington, D.C.

————. 2000. *Interpreting as a discourse process.* New York: Oxford University Press.

Short, K. G., and C. Burke. 1991. *Creating curriculum: Teachers and students as a community of learners.* Portsmouth, N.H.: Heinemann.

Tannen, D. 1979. What's in a frame? Surface evidence for underlying expectations. In *New directions in discourse processing*, ed. R. O. Freedle, 137–81. Norwood, N.J.: Ablex.

Wadensjö, C. 1992. Interpreting as interaction: On dialogue interpreting in immigration hearings and medical encounters. Ph.D. diss., Linköping University, Linköping, Sweden.

————. 1998. *Interpreting as interaction.* New York: Longman.

Yoken, C., ed. 1979. *Interpreter training: State of the art.* Washington, D.C.: The National Academy of Gallaudet College.

ELIZABETH A. WINSTON AND
CHRISTINE MONIKOWSKI

Discourse Mapping

Developing Textual Coherence Skills in Interpreters

SUCCESSFUL INTERPRETATIONS require an in-depth understanding of the underlying coherence of a source language text and the ability to produce an equally coherent message in the target language. This is much more than a superficial recognition of the words or signs; it is the ability to understand a message from multiple perspectives, recognizing the subtle links between the meaning of the message, the context of the message, and the linguistic form that the meaning takes. Discussing language tests, Oller compares these perspectives to windows:

> If language tests were like windows through which language proficiency might be viewed, and if language proficiency were thought of as a courtyard that could be seen from a number of different windows, it would seem that a clearer view of the courtyard is possible through some windows than others. (1979, 64)

Discourse analysis is the study of how communication in any form is structured so that it is socially appropriate as well as meaningfully and linguistically accurate (Hatch 1992, 1). When interpreters attempt to translate a message successfully, they are attempting to render the message with the following:

Much of this article was discussed in a course we taught, "Teaching Foundational Skills in Interpreting: Understanding Coherence through Discourse Mapping." The course included two days of face-to-face and online instruction from October 1996 through April 1997. Many thanks to Karen Malcolm, Elisa Maroney, Annette Miner, and Anna Witter–Merithew.

15

1. Accurate content (themes, topics, and events)
2. Appropriate context (register, settings, speaker's goals, etc.)
3. Appropriate linguistic form (discourse structures, transitions, vocabulary, etc.).

This chapter deals with these three aspects of a message. Each aspect contributes an essential piece of the picture, not separately, but as an integrated whole.

Discourse analysis leads to an awareness of the interdependent perspectives of language. It is the logical approach to processing for interpreters and leads to an understanding of the overall meaning that we must convey, providing a multifaceted view of the source, much as Oller described. Historically, considerable training time is spent on the analysis of words, signs, sentences, and sign production. This leads to a common complaint about new interpreters: They include many facts, but the overall meaning is somehow missing. The missing elements are the coherence of the discourse, the goal of the speaker, and the point of the presentation. The features of language that convey the coherence do not coalesce at the phonological, morphological, or syntactic level; they integrate the text only at the discourse level.

When interpreters take time to analyze discourse and become familiar with the schemas and structures, they are better able to attend to the full message that is being presented and therefore have the potential to render a more effective and comprehensible message. The key lies in finding a way to teach the skill of analyzing discourse that works effectively with the languages we deal with and that applies to all kinds of discourse. Finding the key helps interpreters hone a skill that will serve them when working in any situation with any text. Discourse analysis yields an analysis of the meaning of a text at individual interactions in specific situations and at the linguistic features used to negotiate the interactions.

Discourse mapping, based on discourse analysis, provides a systematic approach for teaching students to analyze a text so they can produce successful, effective interpretations. These interpretations are accurate in content, socially appropriate, and linguistically accurate. Discourse mapping is a technique that teaches students how to develop a mental picture of the meaning structure in any given source text. It helps them reconstruct a similar map in the target language. By creating an actual map of a text, students can see the relationship of its three perspectives: content, context, and form. In addition, it helps students actually visualize the production of the text. It is similar to techniques used in reading and writing instruction, often referred to as concept mapping, mind mapping, or idea mapping (including Anderson–Inman and Zeitz 1993; Schultz 1991; Collins and Quillian 1969).

In this chapter we present an in-depth explanation of the entire process of discourse mapping. We begin with an explanation of the process and then describe each activity and the numerous steps involved in the process. We have provided specific examples from two texts, one in ASL and one in English. We hope that as you read through each section, you will take the time to read the full transcripts, follow the maps given as examples, and come to an understanding of this complicated process.

Discourse Mapping: An Explanation

The goal of discourse mapping is twofold: to identify the overall structures within a text and to create meaningful visual representations of these structures. The visual representation of a complete text allows the student to see how the overall structures within it relate to each other, without depending on words or signs. If discourse analysis is truly the appropriate approach for interpreters, then we must consider how to enhance a student's ability to analyze, and we must provide opportunities to practice this analysis for meaning in a nonthreatening, supportive environment. The dated and unsuccessful educational approach of turning on an audiotape and expecting a student to interpret has taught us the value of time and analysis. Discourse mapping is an actual skill that we can impart to students in the classroom and one that will serve them well in future interpreting situations.

Discourse mapping may be used to develop a variety of skills. It can help students to prepare for comprehension before seeing or hearing a text, providing the student with an opportunity to focus on possible topics, events, and interactants (a brainstorming activity). It can be used to enhance comprehension once students have seen or heard a text, providing them with the opportunity to analyze the structure of the text. This in turn helps students understand the signer's or speaker's intended meaning while also attending to vocabulary and grammatical structures as needed. When used to prepare for producing their own original texts, students can map their own brainstorming. When used with interlingual activities, students can develop possible target language texts that effectively represent the source message. Finally, discourse mapping can help students build their analysis skills by providing them with an opportunity to assess the structure of a text they have produced.

Choosing Texts

One of the first tasks the interpreting instructor must perform is choosing texts that are appropriate for the level and goals of students at different stages of their training. As we begin training, more straightforward texts are appropriate; as students master the skills of interpreting, the texts can become more difficult and complex. The challenge is in choosing texts that are appropriate. Unfortunately, we have few guidelines for choosing: Do we base our choices on vocabulary students already know? Do we pick simple topics told in narrative form (which often turn out to be much more difficult than we ever suspected)? How can we choose texts that will be effective for our students? Too often we choose a text because it "looks good," only to find that for some reason it is completely inappropriate. When we happen to find a text that "works," we use it again and again, possibly without ever having a clear idea of why it works and how to find more such workable texts.

Discourse mapping is a very effective strategy for making these choices. Mapping a text provides us with a clear picture of the underlying structure of that text and of the challenges it poses. Mapping highlights the structure of both interwoven and sequential themes. It lets us analyze the presenter's approach, helping us differentiate between a text that is straightforward (a simple listing of topics, subtopics, and details) and a text that is full of asides, multilevel subtopics, or strategies of suspense and involvement in addition to the basic ideas. Once we have mapped the texts, we can choose those that provide the level of complexity appropriate for our students. And once we have mapped the texts ourselves, we have a ready-made means of evaluating students' work throughout the discourse-mapping process. Our map becomes the basis for determining the adequacy and effectiveness of students' own final productions. It also helps us to better understand the processes students experience or struggle with as they approach the texts.

Intralingual Skills: Comprehension and Production

Once texts are chosen, discourse mapping is an invaluable tool for developing the intralingual skills necessary for comprehending a source text.[1] This works for any source text, whether it is ASL or English. For example, discourse mapping develops comprehension of an ASL text by helping students overcome their tendency to freeze when they see a sign they do not recognize. Discourse mapping leads them to an understanding of the larger context and discourse structures of the text; by understanding these, they can develop analytical skills for zeroing in on the meaning of single vocabulary items. In other words, it helps them understand the meaning rather than the words. If the source text is English, discourse mapping can demonstrate that their initial understanding of the text may be both superficial and inadequate and that a deeper level of understanding is essential to truly interpreting the purpose of the text and the goals of the speaker.

Once students comprehend the meaning of a source text, mapping is effective in developing the visual and auditory perception skills necessary for perceiving the linguistic forms that express this meaning. Students often have great difficulty seeing topic boundaries in an ASL source text. Once they have mapped the topics and goals, however, students can review a text and identify the linguistic features that mark the topic shifts. They begin to see that topic A becomes topic B at the same time that a body shift occurs (or an ASL

---

1. Mapping is effective in introductory ASL courses as well as in interpreter education.

discourse marker appears or a certain combination of eyegaze, head nod, and pausing co-occur). As their perceptive skills grow, they begin to recognize the linguistic forms of ASL as structural elements that express the underlying meaning of the message. Similarly in English, students can begin to recognize the intonation patterns that signal discourse structures such as lists, disagreement, enhanced involvement, and idea boundaries.

Once students understand the meaning and context of a message and recognize the linguistic forms that express that meaning, they can more effectively produce their own messages. Discourse mapping promotes skill growth in this area, both in developing intralingual production skills and later in transitioning to interlingual activities. Students can use the discourse maps from texts they have understood (previous activity) to retell the meaning in their own way in the same language. As they focus on retelling the meaning, they are forced to think about the linguistic forms their retellings will take. Their retellings begin to include both the underlying meaning of the original and the many linguistic features needed to produce a comprehensible target text. When students, for example, understand that head nods are very useful to them in understanding ASL, they tend to use them more frequently in their own productions. The same principle applies to the retelling of English texts in English. An important impact of discourse mapping at this level is that, because all the students are developing both their perceptive and productive skills, they are far more able to provide quality feedback to their peers. This means that students receive increased feedback time during their courses; they do not have to sit and wait until the instructor tells them what is effective and what is not.

Discourse mapping can also help students produce their own original source texts. Often, intralingual activities require students to prepare a text in either ASL or English. Especially when the goal is an ASL text, students often revert to writing the English text, then looking up signs to gloss onto those words. Students are forced to stop thinking about discrete signs when they are first required to develop a map of their text and to think about both the meaning they wish to convey (whether it is a joke or a persuasive argument) and the context in which they intend to situate the text. When they have mapped their text, they can then think about the sequencing of the ideas and the linguistic forms needed to make their texts comprehensible to others.

Interlingual Skill Development

Once students are able to map source texts easily in both ASL and English—first for comprehension and then for intralingual production—they can continue to benefit from discourse mapping as they shift to interlingual exercises, a transition that is difficult at best. At this stage the concept of spiraling in discourse mapping becomes applicable. Using texts that have already been comprehended and then produced in the intralingual exercises, students can transform these texts into the target language. Spiraling eliminates the typical barriers we erect for students and allows them to focus on the single skill of transforming meaning; they are not distracted by the need to also understand the source. Discourse mapping provides a clear understanding of the source, allowing students to work on the target. In addition, they can focus on the underlying meaning in the target and discuss how the target language expresses the meaning. If the source text in ASL is based on a spatial comparison and their analysis of English comparisons indicates that English uses prosody and intonation for the same function, then they know how to effectively produce a similar meaning in the target language.

   The transition to interlingual activities takes advantage of discourse mapping at every step. Students begin translating between ASL and English, building their translations from their discourse maps of the source texts. Once proficient at building translations through discourse mapping, they can progress to consecutive interpreting more easily. They can take in the source text, map it, and, using their internalized skills, map their production in the target language. Discourse mapping is especially effective at this point because here student interpreters so often fall back on word-for-sign glossing, and underlying meaning flies out the window. Interestingly, students who have internalized the mapping process are not satisfied with the output of word-to-sign matching. It no longer makes sense to them to throw out a string of signs just because the speaker said something (or vice versa). Because they see the connections between the topics, the context, the speaker, and the audience (thanks to their training), they are no longer satisfied with just making a connection between a word and a sign. Students transitioning through consecutive and eventually simultaneous interpreting using discourse mapping discuss questions of meaning. They ask "What's the point" of a text or passage? They do not ask "What's the sign for this word?" or "What's the word for that sign?" They are truly learning to interpret.

Determining Equivalence

Finally, discourse mapping becomes an effective tool for evaluating the adequacy of an interpretation. Once a source text has been mapped for underlying meaning, context, and linguistic forms, students transform the text according to this map, thus building these aspects into the target language. Then it is an easy matter to evaluate the transformation, whether it is a translation, a consecutive interpretation, or a simultaneous interpretation. Students (and instructors) can map the resulting target text and compare that map to the source map: Are the meanings, the topics, the interrelationships of ideas, the context, and the goals of the source text apparent in the map of the target text? Does the map reflect the same level of conceptual subtlety, linguistic sophistication, generalities, and specifics of the source map? If so, the transformation is effective; if not, the gaps are usually very clear.

APPLICATION

Our first goal is to introduce you to the texts we will be using and provide a brief summary so you can follow our examples. The first is "Buying My Condo," a text that we refer to throughout the chapter. The second is "Living Fully," an English source text. We recommend that you read the transcripts provided in the appendices and watch the originals, if possible.

In "Buying My Condo," the signer tells the story of how and why he bought a condominium (see Appendix 1). His underlying goal is to share the information and perhaps to entertain an audience, but his underlying approach is to emphasize his luck at the various factors that came together to make the purchase possible. He relates that he has been thinking about buying a place to live and has been looking around but has not been serious about it because he is still in school. He plans to wait until his studies are finished before buying a home but continues to go to open houses, read the classifieds, and ask friends for advice.

As he continues his search, he happens upon the perfect place. He describes its location and appearance. He makes an offer, which is eventually accepted, and then has to deal with financial issues such as getting a mortgage, demonstrating his credit rating, arranging inspections, and so forth. Finally all the paperwork is done, and he moves in. He concludes by saying that he has also finished his studies.

In "Living Fully" (Appendix 2), the speaker provides information in the hopes of inspiring people to have a positive attitude. She begins by introducing herself and her hope that the presentation will be useful. She cites several references related to her topic and then tells a story about a boy talking to three bricklayers. The story illustrates three interpretations of bricklaying: putting bricks down, one on top of the other; putting bricks together to achieve a product (a wall); and striving toward a finished project, a beautiful cathedral. Following this story, she asks the audience which interpretation they prefer and emphasizes that the interpretation affects our outlook as either positive or negative. She discusses the effect of our perceptions and fears on our attitude and further illustrates her point with two more stories. She closes by once again emphasizing that we control our attitudes, and she finishes with a poem to further illustrate her message.

Discourse Mapping Applied to Intralingual Activities

In this section we apply discourse mapping to an actual text and work through the process, step by step. Remember that this process is not meant to be accomplished in a short period of time. Rather, parts of this process can be used in a variety of courses, from the initial brainstorming to completing and evaluating a successful interpretation. In addition, each of these activities should be spread over several class periods, allowing students time to internalize the text as well as the structure of the activity. Each activity is meant to be practiced numerous times with different texts. The point is to teach students the entire process over a period of time. Later in the education process, it is reasonable to expect students to work through the entire process independently.

Comprehension

PREPARATION (BRAINSTORMING)

1. Goals
   a. Students map possible topics, themes, relationships, and events that relate to the given topic.
   b. Students practice discussing this topic with both their peers and the instructor.
2. Objectives
   a. Practice vocabulary related to the given topic.
   b. Build confidence in prediction skills.
   c. Share world knowledge and experiences.
   d. Practice the ability to focus on a specific topic.
   e. Practice assessing language production for accuracy and completeness.
   f. Build confidence in comprehension skills.
   g. Practice discussing a given topic.
   h. Develop feedback skills through discussion of topic and maps with peers and instructor.
   i. Develop feedback skills through discussion of productions and maps with peers and instructor.
3. Discussion

   This mapping activity—done intralingually—prepares the students for comprehension by helping them focus on possible topics.

That is, if the source message is ASL, all class discussions are conducted in ASL (maps are written in English notes or pictures). Having chosen a text ("Buying My Condo"), the instructor might give the topic "real estate" to the class to brainstorm. Students will brainstorm through three levels: (1) content—topics, subtopics, themes, relationships, and events that might occur in that text; (2) context— registers, settings, audiences, and speaker goals for such a text; and (3) form—specific linguistic features of ASL that might be used, including possible vocabulary. Besides creating the visual map with students, this trilevel analysis of a topic presents an opportunity for students to develop their analysis skills. It helps them analyze the meaning of a text without being tied to its sequentiality. At this point, we do not want to know "what happened next." We want to comprehend the meaning.

Step 1. The instructor first selects an appropriate text for this activity (See "Choosing Appropriate Texts."). We have chosen "Buying My Condo."

Step 2. Once the videotape has been selected, the instructor introduces the topic "real estate" to the students but does not show the videotape at this point.

Step 3. Begin the brainstorming activity, eliciting possible subtopics, themes, relationships, and events that may occur in a text related to real estate. In addition, the instructor should elicit student brainstorming regarding the setting, register, and speaker goals that might be associated with such a text. As the students contribute their ideas, the instructor begins to draw a random map on the board, filling in nodes as the students respond. Prompts such as "What might someone talk about if he/she were telling a story related to real estate?" and "Who are specific individuals involved in such a transaction?" are appropriate at this time.

Step 4. Often students focus on content (themes, events, etc.). If the brainstorming peters out, the instructor may prompt the students by asking questions such as "Who might be in the audience?" or " Why would someone tell this story?" This information is included in the random map on the board. (Map 1 is an example of a random map for steps 3 and 4.)

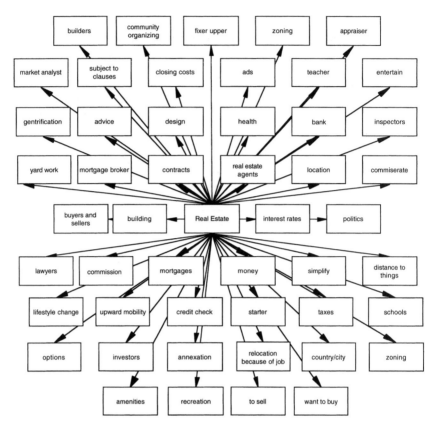

Map 1

Step 5. Now the class discusses linguistic features that convey specific information. For example, the instructor might lead a discussion about the use of space in ASL. "If one were comparing possible residences, which features of ASL might be effective for comparing the asking-price by the sellers?" "If one were to discuss applying for a mortgage, which features of ASL might be effective for conveying the amount of time required to complete such a task?" Discussion should also include the vocabulary a signer might be using for this topic.

Throughout this process, teachers should prompt students to consider subtopics that are not readily mentioned. This activity helps students use their world knowledge, their experiences, and their prediction skills to come up with numerous possibilities. The instructor must also guide the students to the information contained in the selected text (keeping in mind that this is an activity that prepares the students to view that text). Perhaps "Other than apartments and townhouses, what types of residential purchases might a person make?" would elicit the answer "condo" or "house."

The map developed during this activity may appear chaotic, but right now the goal is to identify features from all three levels. The teacher should lead the group the first time this activity is done. Once students understand the activity, it can be assigned as group work, individual work, or homework for subsequent texts. When groups or individuals create maps, they should be shared and compared; sharing everyone's map exposes students to many possible subtopics. Again, the instructor needs to guide this activity so students do not stray too far afield. We want them to be creative, not disconnected. And finally, it is essential to remember that this entire process requires time.

Step 6. When the instructor decides that enough possibilities have been identified, the class begins categorizing the map. For example, the real estate topics could be grouped into the following three categories: finances, people involved in the purchase, and location. We are trying to avoid any kind of sequential categorizing (e.g., first this happened, then this, etc.) and to focus instead on the main themes. (We provide an example of categorizing the topics in a later activity.)

Enhancing Comprehension

1. Goals
   a. Discuss the content, context, and form of an actual text.
   b. Produce a map reflecting comprehension of the topic.
2. Objectives
   a. Identify external aspects of the text (context).
   b. Begin to identify internal structures of the text (content and linguistic forms).
   c. Build confidence in memories of the source text.

   d. Practice analyzing underlying meaning through surface linguistic features.

   e. Build confidence in abilities to analyze meaning.

   f. Practice assessing the source language of others for accuracy and completeness.

   g. Build confidence in their comprehension skills as students discuss their work with the group.

   h. Practice assessing language production for accuracy and completeness.

   i. Develop feedback skills through discussion of productions and maps with peers and instructor.

3. Discussion

The second mapping activity, used to enhance comprehension, builds upon the brainstorm map from the first activity. We continue to address the three aspects of discourse structure: content (topics, events, and relationships); context (setting, register, and speaker's goals); and form (linguistic features and vocabulary).

Step 1. After completing the brainstorming activity, show students the preselected text, "Buying My Condo," looking for content and context.

Step 2. The class now begins to develop a new map that represents actual topics, themes, and relationships (content) as well as setting, register, and speaker's goals (context). As we said before, this activity is best conducted as a class the first time. However, this activity, as well as all the others, needs to be repeated numerous times. Once students understand the activity, it is possible for them to work in small groups. The activity is repeated several times at this level until the map is complete. This not only creates a visual representation of the text but also provides the opportunity for students to recall and organize the text, build confidence in their memories and their ability to make sense of events, and discuss their decisions with their peers. (Maps 2A and 2B demonstrate two different examples of this same process at this point.) The instructor should again guide the students to accuracy.

Step 3. Watch the videotape again.

Step 4. Expand the map, making sure the information about content and context is adequately represented. Repeat until the map is fairly complete.

Step 5. When the instructor decides the map is complete, the class begins to categorize the concepts (see Map 3).

Step 6. Once the map has been categorized, the instructor can focus on form (linguistic features and vocabulary). The students identify or recall the linguistic features used by the signer. For the condo text, these features would include use of space to talk about houses, townhouses, and apartments; use of classifiers to describe the windows in the condo; and use of constructed action and dialogue to show the negotiation for the price. The instructor should also focus on any vocabulary that occurred in the text that might be new to the students. These features can be mapped onto Map 3.

Step 7. Repeat the cycle until the students' maps are complete.

Production: Reconstructing Existing Texts

1. Goals
   a. Using their own mental constructs, students produce meaningful texts that contain the content and meaning of the source.
   b. Practice assessing the language for accuracy and completeness.
2. Objectives
   a. Build confidence in production skills.
   b. Build confidence in comprehension skills (each time students watch another person's story, they build comprehension skills).
   c. Practice producing underlying meaning through surface linguistic features.
   d. Practice assessing productions for accuracy and completeness.
   e. Practice assessing others' productions for same.
   f. Build confidence in abilities to analyze meaning.
   g. Build confidence in memories for the source text.
   h. Practice analyzing underlying meaning through surface linguistic features.

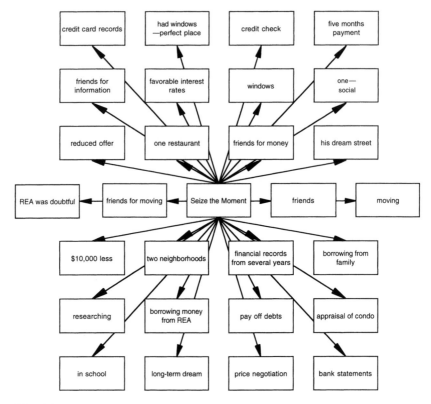

Map 2A

i. Continue practicing mapping (i.e., analyzing meaning and linguistic forms).
j. Develop feedback skills through discussion of productions and maps with peers and instructor.

3. Discussion

To summarize, students have completed the first two activities, brainstorming and enhancing comprehension of the topic. Students now have a visual map of the content, context, and form used in the original text (Map 3). The instructor can now continue to the next step—production. This is still an intralingual activity, asking the students to retell the source text in their own way.

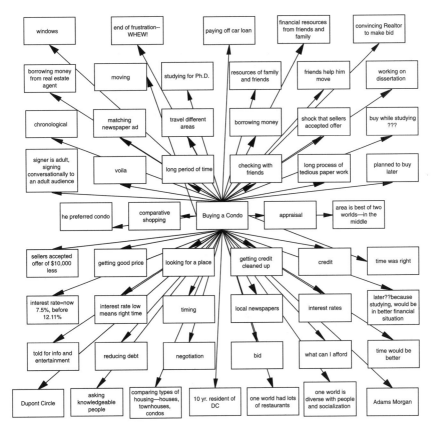

Map 2B

Production is most effective if students are not permitted to see the source text (video) again at this point. This forces them to produce a text with the same meaning but using their own mental constructs, skills, and abilities to express those same meanings. This helps them to make the meaning their own and allows them to play with their productions.

Step 1. Working solely from their own maps (activity #2), students prepare their own signed presentation of the material, making sure that the presentation includes the content, context, and appropriate linguistic features. They prepare a sequential map that visually represents the sequential structure of their own presentation.

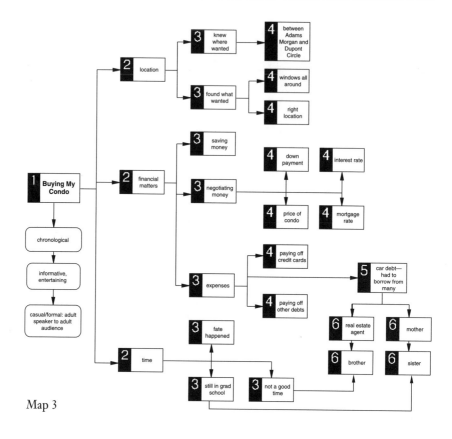

Map 3

Based on previous maps, at this stage such a map lists each feature, topic, and so on in the order the student intends to use for retelling. Using the condo text as our base, one student might sequence the text by doing the following:

1. Describing the condo
2. Describing its location
3. Explaining why it is perfect for the buyer
4. Discussing the financial hassle.

Another student may focus more on the timing aspect of the text, starting with the following:

1. The condo becoming available
2. The buyer leaping at the chance
3. Issues of negotiation.

This sequential map should be fleshed out for the entire text.

Step 2. Once the internal ordering of the text is prepared, students can focus on the linguistic features to be used in producing the text. Next to each segment of their sequential map, they should explain the linguistic features they intend to use in retelling the text. For example, one student may choose to use classifiers to describe the condo features:

CONDO, WINDOW+++, BIG-WINDOW, THERE, THERE, THERE, WOW.

Another may prefer to describe it lexically, adding emphasis by using facial expressions instead of classifiers.

CONDO HAVE MANY WINDOW++, SUN, BRIGHT, PERFECT!

These two productions demonstrate each person's understanding of the source text's discussion of the windows in the condo. One person has understood that the benefit of having lots of windows is the light, whereas another has simply commented on the number of windows, leaving the watcher to fill in the reason the windows are important. A third student may sign something about having a view.

Step 3. Once the students have prepared their retelling maps, they practice the retelling until they can do it comfortably. Students then present their own renditions to others (whether this is to the instructor for a grade, to another student for feedback, or on videotape for self-assessment is a matter for the instructor to decide; each approach will be used at different times during this activity). This exercise again points out the variety of different understandings any interpretation may represent. As students see each variation, they can be directed to discuss the adequacy of the variations:

• Which ones are closer to the source text and why?
• Which ones have been too specific or too general and why?
• What underlying assumptions did the signer have that influenced her or his particular retelling of the text?

This type of discussion helps students hone their skills in understanding source texts at the level of meaning. Rarely do students discuss which sign they chose; usually they discuss the effectiveness of classifiers versus lexical signs for conveying the idea of "great windows," which works better to show emphasis, or better yet, which works more effectively in a particular style of retelling.

One valuable benefit of this retelling from the discourse maps is that students see a variety of appropriate retellings and begin to accept that there is more than one way to accurately represent a message. This frees them from the narrow view they often have that "If the signer used that sign, then I have to say that word" and helps them to develop a broader understanding of the meaning of the original text.

Step 4. Once students have retold the text, it is a simple matter to assess its accuracy. The retelling is compared to: 1) their own map to determine whether they actually included everything they intended to include; and 2) their maps of the original text (activity #2) to determine whether they have included everything they needed to include from the original text. (Determining equivalency by comparing maps is discussed in more detail later.)

Discourse Mapping Applied to Interlingual Exercises

Translation

Once students have become adept at mapping texts for comprehension and for production as intralingual activities, they are ready to move on to interlingual activities. As we have already stressed, students are expected to practice these activities on several texts over a period of time, internalizing the process of analyzing meaning one step at a time. Once they have mastered the intralingual mapping skills in both English and ASL, they are ready to focus on transforming that meaning from one language into the other. In this section we discuss the progression from intralingual to interlingual, and we outline the process from translation to simultaneous interpretation.

1. Goal: Students produce accurate and complete target texts based on source text discourse maps.

2. Objectives
   a. Review maps of ASL source text and review maps of students' own retelling of text.
   b. Analyze the most effective sequencing and discourse structures for presenting the message in the target language.
   c. Analyze the most effective linguistic features for presenting the target text.
   d. Build confidence in memory, analysis skills, feedback skills, and production skills.
3. Discussion

Teachers can approach the progression from intralingual to interlingual exercises using discourse mapping in two ways. First, students can translate the original text using the discourse maps created in activity #2; second, students can translate their own retellings using their discourse maps from activity #3. As always, the goal in these exercises is to lead the students through one step at a time, building incrementally on their previous skills. One way to achieve this is to spiral and recycle materials. Students begin translations by working from texts whose meaning they have already mastered; they use texts that they have already mapped. This way they are only focusing on the process of translation and not also dealing with the process of comprehension and production. Asking students to comprehend, translate, and produce in one giant step from the beginning is not effective; even combining two steps makes the task overwhelming. Consistently adding one step at a time helps them internalize and master each step, so that as they move on, they have confidence in their abilities.

At this stage students should still not review the source text but continue to work from their maps. This helps them avoid the pitfall of glossing and falling back into the "signs" rather than relying on meaning.

Step 1. Using the map of the source text (activity #2), students review the concepts, structures, and linguistic forms they have outlined as they occurred in ASL.

Step 2. Students prepare a sequential map of the original source text (Map 4A, column 1). This map represents the actual order of the original condo text.

Step 3. Students analyze the specific linguistic features associated with each step of the sequential map. (In the condo text, the linguistic features might look like Map 4A, column 2.) In the section of text mapped here, the signer uses space to describe why he likes the location of the condo. He sets up two different neighborhoods, describing the benefits of each one. As he does this, he adds more facial expression. The use of space and facial expression adds emphasis to this segment, drawing the watcher into the telling of the event. Following this segment, the signer mentions that he was reading the newspaper and found a place in that very area. For this segment he continues to use space for emphasis and detail, but he switches to a different type of spatial map. He uses constructed action and monologue to demonstrate his actions and thoughts. Each segment of the sequential map is analyzed for the accompanying linguistic features.

In the "Living Fully" text, the sequential and linguistic feature map might look like Map 4B. The speaker uses ellipsis and poetic language to build involvement. She employs rhetorical questions often, and she uses sentence and paragraph structures that recur, a technique used by orators to build rhythm and a sense of continuity within a text. When she describes the boy talking to each bricklayer, she uses the same type of sentence.

> A little boy happened by and asked a question of the first brickmason. The little boy approached the second brickmason and asked him the same thing. The little boy approached the third brickmason and asked the same question again.

This recurrence of similar form and vocabulary is intentional; it builds structure for the audience. The brickmasons' answers are also structured in similar patterns; each is described by where he looks and then by what he says (I'm . . . , I'm . . . , I am . . .). The major difference in these three sections of the story lies in the way each bricklayer ends the final sentence. One finishes with "I'm laying brick" (intonation is somewhat sarcastic and dismissive); one with "I'm

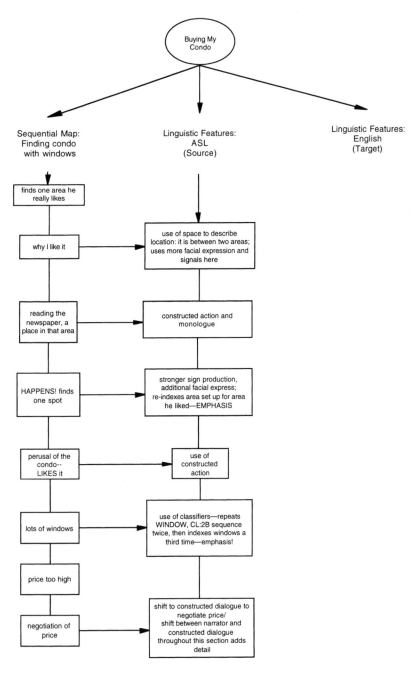

Buying My Condo

Sequential Map:
Finding condo
with windows

Linguistic Features:
ASL
(Source)

Linguistic Features:
English
(Target)

finds one area he
really likes

why I like it

use of space to describe
location: it is between two areas;
uses more facial expression and
signals here

reading the
newspaper, a
place in that area

constructed action and
monologue

HAPPENS! finds
one spot

stronger sign production,
additional facial express;
re-indexes area set up for area
he liked—EMPHASIS

perusal of the
condo--
LIKES it

use of
constructed
action

lots of windows

use of classifiers—repeats
WINDOW, CL:2B sequence
twice, then indexes windows a
third time—emphasis!

price too high

negotiation of
price

shift to constructed dialogue to
negotiate price/
shift between narrator and
constructed dialogue
throughout this section adds
detail

Map 4A

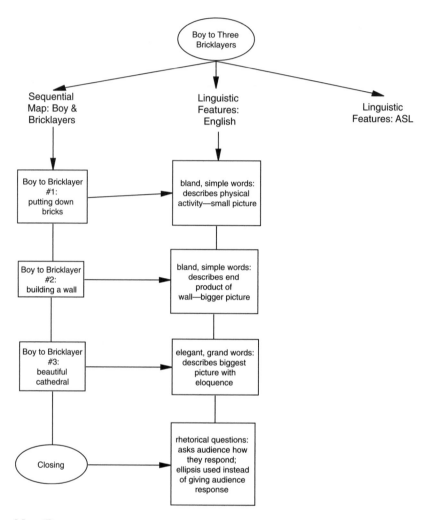

Map 4B

building a wall" (ordinary intonation); and one with "I am building a beautiful cathedral" (the speaker uses the word *pride* and also adds pride to her voice). The speaker does not comment on these differences; she leaves the audience to interpret the point of her story by their recognition of both the redundancies of most of the text and the clear differences in the final sentences.

Step 4. Students begin to determine which English structures will achieve the same results (Map 5A, column 3). Because the signer used space and facial expression for added emphasis and detail, an English rendition might need to include descriptive adjectives as well as intonation and stress.

We also provide an example of this step for the English text, "Living Fully" (see Map 5B). When the boy is talking to the first bricklayer, where the English words are bland, the signed rendition might use constructed dialogue with little additional facial expression. When the boy talks to the second bricklayer, the signed sentence might be very similar, especially because the source sentence structures are similar (as noted earlier). The signed rendition of the question to the third bricklayer would need to continue the use of constructed dialogue to portray this intended parallel.

The result of this exercise is a map representing the internal structure and the linguistic features of the target text that effectively represents the source text.

Step 5. Once this map is ready, students produce the target version. When working from the condo text, the target version might be in written English. The goal for a written translation would be to focus primarily on the appropriate register, vocabulary selection, and major discourse structures (such as time passage, comparisons, and performatives). Or the translation may be directly into spoken English, focusing on voice production, intonation, stress, pitch, and so on, as well as structure. When the preparation for the translation is completed, students practice it and present it (as in previous activities).

Step 6. The presentation is assessed for both accuracy and completeness. This can be done by mapping the presented text and comparing that map to the one used to prepare the translation (from activity #3).

A variation of this activity is to have the students prepare a translation from the maps produced in activity #3 from their own retellings of the source text. Once they have prepared and presented these translations, it is beneficial for students to compare their translation of the source text and their translation of their own retelling. This comparison points out clearly those ideas that have been lost along the way, the ones that have remained, and the places where students need to refocus their efforts. Students whose maps

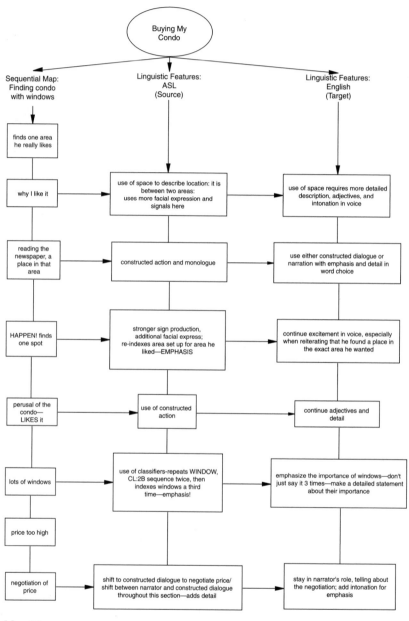

Buying My Condo

Sequential Map: Finding condo with windows
- finds one area he really likes
- why I like it
- reading the newspaper, a place in that area
- HAPPEN! finds one spot
- perusal of the condo—LIKES it
- lots of windows
- price too high
- negotiation of price

Linguistic Features: ASL (Source)
- use of space to describe location: it is between two areas: uses more facial expression and signals here
- constructed action and monologue
- stronger sign production, additional facial express; re-indexes area set up for area he liked—EMPHASIS
- use of constructed action
- use of classifiers-repeats WINDOW, CL:2B sequence twice, then indexes windows a third time—emphasis!
- shift to constructed dialogue to negotiate price/ shift between narrator and constructed dialogue throughout this section—adds detail

Linguistic Features: English (Target)
- use of space requires more detailed description, adjectives, and intonation in voice
- use either constructed dialogue or narration with emphasis and detail in word choice
- continue excitement in voice, especially when reiterating that he found a place in the exact area he wanted
- continue adjectives and detail
- emphasize the importance of windows—don't just say it 3 times—make a detailed statement about their importance
- stay in narrator's role, telling about the negotiation; add intonation for emphasis

Map 5A

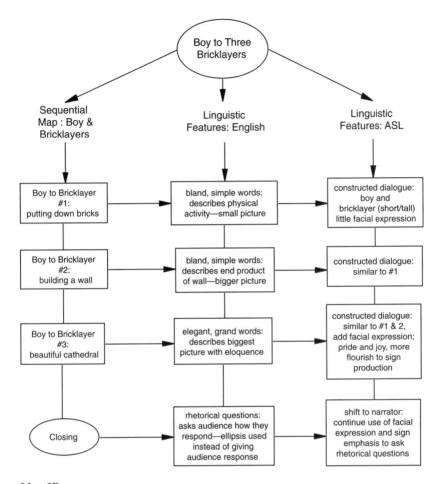

Map 5B

have been accurate and complete at each stage of the process should have translations that are elegant, well formed, complete, and accurate, albeit very different in the surface linguistic forms. Students whose maps have strayed from preceding maps will find gaps in their final translations and topics or details that range from completely lost to minimally distorted. This analysis leads to a greater awareness of effective translations.

The step from intralingual retelling exercises to interlingual translation exercises has traditionally been a difficult one for students. Using discourse mapping, students make the transition one step at a time, always working with underlying meaning to understand the message and transform it. However, this process also focuses on the surface linguistic structures, helping students perceive the subtle linguistic strategies used to produce underlying meaning. In the next section we discuss the transition from translation to consecutive interpreting using discourse mapping as a tool.

Consecutive Interpreting

1. Goals
   a. Transition from translation to consecutive interpreting
   b. Develop techniques that build skills and confidence
2. Objectives
   a. Preparation
      (1) Develop discourse maps of texts within a time limit
      (2) Produce sequential discourse maps of source texts within a time limit
      (3) Prepare translations based on sequential discourse maps within a time limit; assess translations
      (4) Chunk the translations within a time limit.
   b. Performance
      (1) Perform the chunked translations within a time limit
      (2) Assess the chunked translations
   c. Using new source texts, apply the preceding process to new texts.
3. Discussion

The first part of this activity is preparation. If students have internalized the process of transforming a message from language to another, then the biggest change from the previous activity, translation, to consecutive interpreting should be the change from an unlimited to a limited time for preparation and production of texts. Because one goal is always to limit the number of new steps when advancing from stage to stage, it is important that students enter into consecutive interpreting facing first the challenge of time, without also facing the challenge of processing and producing new text. For this, we start once again with the texts mapped during activities.

Step 1. Discuss goals and objectives of this activity. At this stage students should review the actual source text. Continuing with the example of the condo text, the teacher introduces the goals of the activity and leads students through a review of the mapping process.

Step 2. Prepare a discourse map of the text within a limited time. Begin this step by showing the source text to the class. Give students 10 minutes to produce a discourse map of themes, ideas, and so on. These maps will not be as detailed as the original maps from activity #2 but should include the major features and supporting information. This activity adds the pressure of time without adding the fear of not understanding the source text.

Step 3. Students view the source text again and have another 5–10 minutes to categorize the ideas.

Step 4. Sequence the text within a time limit (5–20 minutes). Once they have mapped the text, they need to sequence the items on their maps in the order they occur in the source text.

Step 5. List the linguistic features occurring at each sequenced chunk within a time limit. Students list the linguistic features used in the source text for each chunk of the sequential map. Our suggested time limit is 15–30 minutes. (The results would be similar to Map 5A.)

Step 6. Assess sequential maps for accuracy and completeness. This step can be done as a class, by the instructor, or through small-group discussion. Assessment is based on the discourse maps produced during activity #2, the original mapping of the source text. Successful completion of this activity builds student confidence in their abilities to analyze source texts more and more quickly.

Step 7. Prepare a translation based on the sequential map within a limited time. Once the sequential and linguistic feature map is prepared, students begin building the translation. Much of this will be familiar because the students have already worked intensively with this text. However, the forms of the target language may be very different; students should thus be encouraged to produce a translation based on the map produced during this activity rather than trying to remember how they did it the last time. Thus, their translation of the condo text may be very different from the one they prepared for the previous translation activity. Suggested limit for the first time is 30 minutes. This time limit can be increased if necessary but should be progressively decreased with subsequent texts.

Step 8. Chunking the translation. Once the translation is prepared, the teacher introduces the next step—chunking the material into meaningful sections for consecutive interpreting. These sections should include full ideas and should be of some length (four to five idea units). The goal is to have students learn where and how to chunk larger texts. Discourse mapping is useful at this stage; students can usually use their maps to find the meaningful sections of the text.

Step 9. Consecutive interpreting/unlimited production time. When the text has been translated and chunked, students can begin the next step—consecutive interpreting. The source text should be prepared so that it is paused at each chunk; students can pause the tape, they can cue a partner to pause the tape, or they can edit the tape so that there is a pause in it (much easier technically for audio- than videotape). During the initial consecutive interpreting, students are allowed as long a pause as they need to present their interpretation of the chunk. The source text is not restarted until they have finished. (It is assumed that they are adept at this interpretation and are not repeating, repairing, and otherwise stumbling along during this pause.)

Step 10. Consecutive interpreting/limited production time. Once students are comfortable with consecutively interpreting with self-regulated pausing, the next step is to introduce another time constraint. This time the time constraint is the length of the pause between chunks. To begin, it is often effective if the pause is slightly longer than is needed to take a few seconds to think and then say the interpretation. This adds pressure to the students' task while still allowing them to produce successful interpretations without falling behind. As the students' comfort level increases, the pause length is shortened until the students are still interpreting while the next chunk is presented. At first this overlap should be just small enough to provide students with the experience of taking in information while also producing it. (Students should also have had exposure to multitasking activities before moving into this level of consecutive interpreting.) It is important that students wait to begin each chunk until they have heard it all.

In consecutive interpreting, the pauses never completely disappear. An end step for this activity is to have 5-second pauses between chunks. Students are viewing the new chunks while producing the old ones but know that they have fixed places for pulling themselves back together. As students become comfortable with this activity, it is useful to have them chunk the tapes according to their own needs. This helps build their confidence in their chunking abilities and their ability to deal with a variety of pacing approaches. Once students have chunked their source texts, they can share them with their peers and practice consecutively interpreting each other's texts.

Step 11. Assess production. When students have done their consecutive interpretation of a text, they return to the mapping process to evaluate the effectiveness of their interpretations. They map the target text, comparing that map with that made of the source text. This comparison points out clearly the areas needing improvement, and so on. Students may also practice mapping each other's target texts and giving feedback to their peers about the productions.

As a form of assessment at this point, teachers may want to evaluate the target production for accuracy and completeness (comparing the students' text to the teacher's own map of the source text) and also evaluate the students' ability to self-assess by comparing the students' source and target maps. In this way students learn not only what they did on a particular text but also how to assess their own performances, a skill they need for continued development once they leave the program.

The third part of this activity includes the introduction of new texts. As we have stressed before, it is important to work through this process with known texts, adding only one new step at a time. When students have learned this process, the instructor can start again with new texts, beginning first with a viewing, then working swiftly through each activity (mapping, retelling, translating, consecutively interpreting, and finally simultaneously interpreting). Even when preparing a new text, students should turn in a completed mapping assignment before they begin to consecutively interpret the text. No new text should be consecutively interpreted until this is completed. Again, we are reinforcing the goal of preparation and of internalizing the process until it becomes second nature to the students.

Simultaneous Interpreting

Discourse mapping at this stage is applied to assessment of interpretations that have been prepared throughout the process. This activity brings the student to actual simultaneous interpreting.

1. Goal: Students transition from the activity of consecutive interpreting to simultaneous interpreting
2. Objectives
   a. Using texts previously mapped and performed, eliminate pausing between chunks while interpreting
   b. Using the mapping process, prepare and produce simultaneous interpretations of new texts.
3. Discussion

Step 1. Transition from consecutive to simultaneous interpretation using previously prepared texts. At this stage, the transition from consecutive to simultaneous interpreting is a matter of eliminating the pauses in the source text. By using the prepared texts, students are faced with learning only how to work under the new time constraint at the early stages of this activity.

Step 2. Preparation and performance of new texts. Once they are able to comfortably interpret prepared texts, students can begin to work on new texts simultaneously. Of course, they should prepare each text following each step of the process before they simultaneously interpret until the process becomes second nature. When this happens, students will be able to chunk texts into meaningful sections and provide interpretations with little apparent need for the mapping process (it is happening quickly and internally). Having internalized the process, they continue to think in terms of underlying meaning and not in terms of specific signs or words. Their interpretations are just that: meaningful target texts rather than strings of signs.

Step 3. Assessment. Simultaneous interpreting performances are assessed for accuracy and completeness by the instructor, peers, or student self-assessment. Again, it is important to emphasize that these assessments are intended to identify patterns of weakness and processing problems. They are not intended to be assessments of the product alone but of the process and the product both.

Evaluating Equivalence

The first problem with determining equivalence is that it leads one to believe there is only one right way to interpret a text. For too long we have worked under the impression that an interpreter produces either a "good" or a "bad" message, meaning that one has either accomplished the task or not. To speak of equivalence implies that complete equivalence is an achievable goal, although in reality it is a relative term, that of the closest approximation to the source language meaning. The terms "effective" or "successful" are perhaps more useful concepts. "Adequacy of a given translation [and interpretation] can . . . be judged in terms of the specifications of the particular translation to be performed and in terms of the user's [or consumer's] needs" (Hatim and Mason 1990, 8). The focus of assessing equivalence "is the extent to which the intent of the source is comprehended by the receptors" (Nida 1977). Larson's view of assessment in translation requires answers to three questions (which follow Nida's classic "basic requirements" of a translation [1964, 164]): Is the meaning of the target language the same as that of the source language? Is the message clearly understood by the audience for whom the message was intended? Is the form natural? (Larson 1984, 49) These three questions serve interpreters well and quite clearly encompass our view of an effective interpretation; they certainly support the sociocultural context in which all equivalence must be assessed (Hatim and Mason 1990, 12). We must always go back to the consumers to assess the effectiveness of our work, but first we must assess the process that leads us to that product. Discourse mapping supports the assessment of that process. The problem with determining equivalence of an interpreted or translated message is that "the target text displays only the translator's [interpreter's] final decisions . . . in other words, we are looking at translations as product instead of . . . as process" (2). However, by creating discourse maps in a step-by-step, methodical way, instructors can monitor the process the student is experiencing and therefore have an impact on those steps rather than only assessing the equivalence of the finished product.

The holistic/gestalt approach to assessing our students' work is also supported by Hatim and Mason in their discussion of "effectiveness and efficiency" in translation:

> The judgments that text producers make about what can be assumed to be shared with text receivers often exert a determining influence on the form an emerging text will take. . . . The balance is regulated by the principles of effectiveness (achieving maximum transmission of relevant content of fulfillment of a communicative goal) and efficiency (achieving it in the most economical way, involving minimum expenditure of processing effort). Thus, the guiding principle for deciding what to include in a text and what to take for granted may be stated as: Is the gain in effectiveness sufficient to warrant the extra processing effort involved? (1990, 93)

The questions now become the following: How can discourse mapping be applied to these approaches to determining equivalence? and How can the work that is produced throughout the process be assessed?

First of all, at each step, it is the instructor's responsibility to elicit responses that will support the finished product. The instructor knows both the text and the students; therefore, he or she needs to keep the students focused, without narrowing their participation too much. This is closely tied to selecting an appropriate text in the first place. We want students to use their processing skills, their world knowledge, and their proficiency in both English and ASL to work through their mapping activities. But we also want these activities to be successful. This is not to imply that they are error-free activities, but it serves no purpose to allow students to go too far afield with their work. It is incumbent upon the instructor to guide students to success in these activities because those successes build upon each other to create a confident interpreter. Gone are the days when we required students to voice a videotape "cold."

Second, again it is the instructor's responsibility to assess the maps at each step. We have, throughout this chapter, emphasized the fact that this process is an ongoing, long-term approach to interpreting. Numerous steps of the mapping process need to be repeated on an "as needed" basis until the instructor believes the map to be complete. Students should not be allowed to breeze through these activities with incomplete maps or incomplete understanding of the steps. This applies to the instructor as well. The instructor must create maps for all the steps prior to introducing the activity to the class. This requires quite a bit of time "up front," but it will also ensure a smooth and coherent process as the course/semester/program unfolds. Not only will this preparation guide the instructor (and therefore make the students' work more productive), but it will also give the instructor tools with which equivalence can be assessed. At last we have a tangible, visual tool with which we can compare steps in the process. For example, take the map you created for activity #2 (see Map 2A) and compare it with those the students created. How complete are their maps? Did they include enough/too many details? Did they include something you missed? You may notice perhaps that several students insist upon retaining some of the subtopics from the original brainstorming map despite their irrelevance. It would be best to remind the students that this information, although potentially appropriate, was deemed to be extraneous to this particular story and should not be included in this map. Or, during activity #4 (see Map #4A), a student might not have included use of space as a linguistic feature that supports the reasons the speaker likes that particular condo. The instructor could direct the student to include that feature; this might be an appropriate time to have a discussion about the use of space in ASL. It may be beneficial to the entire class to have a bit of a review and practice session on this particular linguistic feature. All of this information can be elicited from the students' maps as the instructor compares them.

Third, the instructor must also lead the students to assess their own work as appropriate. A sense of completeness must be achieved at each step. For many of the activities just outlined, it is appropriate for students to work in small groups. Perhaps assigning a specific map to be completed over a 1-week period would allow three or four students to work together first as a team and then come together as an entire class. This approach supports a number of the goals we established for each lesson including the following: develop feedback skills through discussion of topic and maps with peers and instructor; develop feedback skills through discussion of productions and maps with peers and instructor; and build confidence in their abilities to analyze meaning. During activity #5 (consecutive interpreting), students can practice mapping each other's target texts and compare them with the instructor's (Maps 5A and 5B), which will clearly show the areas that are successful and those that still need more work.

Keeping in mind Larson's (1984) three questions for assessing a translation or interpretation, one can seek answers to these questions at specific points in the mapping process. It may not be appropriate for the students to answer each question at every step, but it is appropriate for the instructor to do so (because the instructor knows the text). The first question—Is the meaning of the target language the same as that of the source language?—should be answered for each map created (except for the initial one created for the brainstorming activity), regardless of whether one is working intralingually or interlingually. This question needs to be modified when working intralingually, but the concept of this level of assessment is the same: Is the meaning of the source language accurately represented on this map? For example, let us look at "Buying a Condo" from activity #2 (enhancing comprehension). Map 3A represents one possible map that could be created during this activity, depicting three subtopics in the narrative: time, location, and financial matters. This is not the only accurate visual representation of the text, but it certainly is a successful one. If one follows this train of thought, then the additional details under each subtopic make sense and support the text. Again, our purpose is not to steer the students to strictly follow the source text; creativity and flexibility are important, but it is not helpful to anyone if students are allowed to go too far afield.

Larson's second question—Is the message clearly understood by the audience for whom the message was intended?—could also be applied at every step beyond the brainstorming session. At this point students should begin to take a more active role in assessing their own maps. When students are creating their discourse maps (beginning with the second activity), they must begin to assess whether classmates understand the message. We expect students' maps to be different, but there is a distinction between different and incomprehensible. There is only so much information being analyzed; most maps will represent quite a bit of similar information at all levels (i.e., vocabulary, settings, and linguistic features).

And Larson's third question—Is the form natural?—can also be applied at every step. When students begin retelling the story in their own words (still working intralingually in the third activity), the question of naturalness should be addressed.

Choosing Appropriate Texts

Now that we have worked through the entire process of mapping, we return to the discussion of how to choose appropriate texts. First, it is important to choose complete texts, texts that have a beginning and an end, and not texts that are extracted from longer texts. Using an unfinished text does not allow the students to analyze the full structure needed for comprehension. Second, it is important at the beginning of each activity to use texts that can be easily finished during a class period. Generally texts of approximately 5 minutes, such as the condo text, work well. When students are working in groups or independently, it is possible to use longer texts such as "Living Fully," which is approximately 15 minutes long. Third, it is essential that students have adequate access to the texts. Students need to be able to work on the texts often and in depth. One or two copies on reserve in the media center may be insufficient; try to have multiple copies available. Whenever possible, students should have their own copies.[2]

On the surface, both "Buying My Condo" and "Living Fully" are fairly straightforward, one point following another. Both presenters are trying to keep the audiences involved and interested. In the condo text, the signer describes buying the condo, including his emotions about the experience. This encourages the audience to re-member their own similar experiences, getting them to be more in-terested in his story. As he describes each event, he adds comments about his feelings: He liked the condo; he was frustrated with the financial dealings; he took a risk when he made the offer to buy. Each event is accompanied by an emotion. The discourse map of "Buying My Condo" (Map 6A) shows underlying meaning structure that is fairly clear and discrete. Each topic has subtopics and details, but there is very little overlap or interweaving of the topics; each one is a unit unto itself. In the sequential map, each of these units occurs in a clear and easily understood chronological order. And we can see when and where ASL features such as constructed dialogue, mono-logue, and action, comparisons, affect, and narrator shift occur and are used to encourage involvement by the audience. Although each of these features is complex in itself, they rarely overlap. Therefore, as we move to the linguistic map of the interpretation (target text), we would expect to find a fairly similar, straightforward English ren-dition with added complexity when features such as constructed di-alogue occur.

In "Living Fully," discourse mapping reveals a completely differ-ent structure and different style of producing involvement. On the sample map (Map 6B), the underlying theme is "You make a differ-ence." The approach to this entire presentation is to compare two

---

2. We are certainly not encouraging making illegal copies; we do encourage the use of tapes and texts that allow students adequate access for analysis.

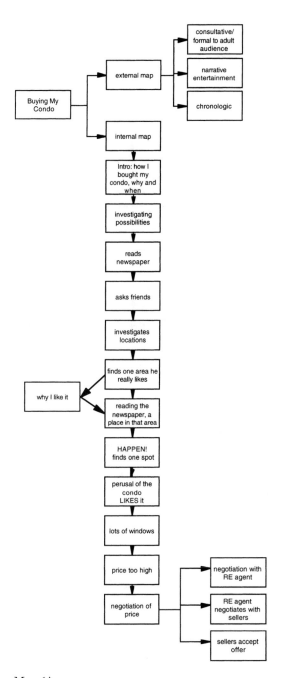

Map 6A

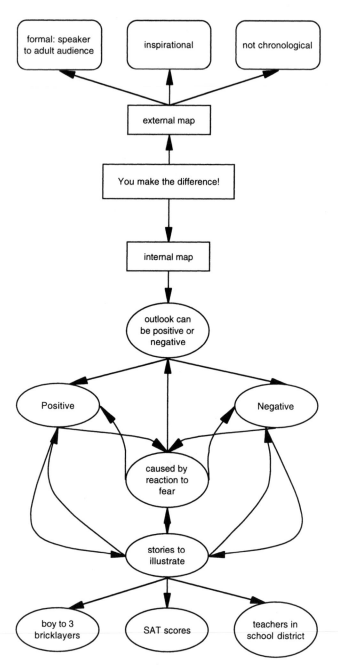

Map 6B

types of interpretations, negative and positive, and to understand how we come to those interpretations. Although in the recounting, each point follows the previous, each point in fact is interwoven with the main point and the comparison. Each story is intimately tied to both the positive and the negative, and both reflect differing interpretations of fear in people's lives. The underlying structure is a richly interwoven fabric, and the discourse map clearly reflects this.

When we analyze the maps for these two stories, the difference is clear in two places. First the overall map of the condo story has clearly separated topics and details, presented for information and entertainment. The "Living Fully" text has a highly interwoven structure, presented for information and inspiration. But there are additional differences as well.

In "Buying My Condo," the narrator uses space frequently, using constructed dialogue, monologue, and action throughout, as well as classifiers and physical locations. An English interpretation will need to represent these features accurately. For example, the use of space indicates more focus on a topic or character, as well as more descriptive detail and vocal intonation, than straight narrative. However, as complex as this may be, it is still a straightforward production. The narrator rarely refers to any previous topics or spaces that represent them. Once he has finished with the search, he does not go back to that, so the spaces he uses for that topic are "erased" for the next topic. There is little comparison, and it occurs within small subtopics (comparing two sections of the city and comparing apartments, houses, and townhouses). These comparisons are not part of the underlying structure of the full text. And the sign use is ordinary everyday conversation. In the final analysis, this text is fairly straightforward and uncomplicated, requiring an understanding of several uses of space but rarely including anything either interwoven or overlapped.

In contrast, the "Living Fully" text is filled with recurring vocal and structural patterns. We focus here on a single section of this text as an example. When the boy talks to the three bricklayers, we hear each bricklayer's answers, but the point, or the focus, is not on the bricklayers and their comments. The real focus is on the attitudes reflected about the same activity. The speaker uses intonation and word choice along with sentence and paragraph structures to focus on the possible attitude rather than on the people or the activity. When we get to the translation and a mapping of possible linguistic features to include, we see that, although constructed dialogue is appropriate to reflect the conversation, the real point needs to be made by adding facial expression and elegance of sign production. This section of text was chosen because so often interpreters miss the point of the section. Once they have heard that there are three different conversations, many interpreters immediately hold three conversations in three different areas, using three different spaces, one for each conversation. They place tremendous emphasis on the fact that the conversations happened rather than on the points made in those conversations. By using a single placement for the boy and by having each bricklayer talk to him, this emphasis is reduced, and the audience can focus on the content of the conversation rather than its simple occurrence.

Having mapped these two texts for ourselves, we can compare the underlying content structures, the context interrelationships, the linguistic features of the source, and the possible/probable (and improbable) target language structures. Once we have this information, choosing texts for students becomes easier, and the chosen texts are more likely to meet the needs and abilities of our students.

SUMMARY

This chapter describes a systematic approach to the application of discourse mapping throughout an interpreter education program. We have outlined six discourse mapping activities and provided an explanation of each activity and detailed instructions for teaching each activity with sample maps from both ASL and English texts.

As educators, we are responsible for guiding our students through the complex process of producing a successful, effective interpretation. This is not an easy task, but it can be done. To be successful, students need to grasp the coherence of the discourse, the goal of the speaker, and the point of the presentation. And they need to produce an integrated whole as a result. Although the phonological, morphological, and syntactic levels of the text are important for comprehension, these features are integrated only at the discourse level, where coherence can be achieved. If students understand the true meaning of the message, the probability of producing a successful interpretation increases greatly.

The ultimate goal of discourse mapping is to give students a complete process that they can actually apply to the interpretation of any text. As teachers, we hope that once the students work through the process a number of times, they will be able to work through all the maps on their own. With practice, the process becomes internalized and automatic. However, this process cannot be rushed. We suggest that this approach to interpreting be integrated throughout the courses in an interpreting program.

Discourse analysis is a way to look at the meaning of the context and how individuals interact in given situations. A successful interpretation takes these aspects of analysis into account. But the leap from discourse analysis to interpretation is a complicated one. Discourse mapping provides a systematic approach for analyzing texts that ultimately lead to interpretations that are accurate for content, socially appropriate and linguistically accurate. The act of viewing a text through the three different "windows": the content (possible topics, subtopics, themes, relationships, and events), the context (registers, settings, audiences, and speaker goals), and the form (specific linguistic features)—provides much more than a superficial recognition of words or signs. It provides students with an analysis of a text and a visual representation that they can rely on to support their interpretations. The process of interpreting becomes less elusive. The view of the courtyard, the source text, becomes clearer and more complete for the student; the view of the courtyard is thereby clearer and more complete for the audience. Discourse mapping is a process that leads to effective interpretations—a result that is, after all, our ultimate goal.

REFERENCES

Anderson-Inman, L., and L. Zeitz. 1993. Computer-based concept mapping: Active studying for active learners. *The Computing Teacher*, August/September, 6–10.

Buying a condo. 1993. Produced by Gallaudet University, Washington, D.C. Videocassette.

Collins, A. M., and M. Ross Quillian. 1969. Retrieval time from semantic memory. *Journal of Verbal Learning and Verbal Behavior* 8:240–47.

Hatch, E. 1992. *Discourse and language education.* Cambridge: Cambridge University Press.

Hatim, B., and I. Mason. 1990. *Discourse and the translator.* London/New York: Longman.

Larson, M. 1984. *Meaning-based translation: A guide to cross-language equivalence.* Lanham, Md.: University Press of America.

Nida, E. A. 1964. *Toward a science of translating with special reference to principles and procedures involved in Bible translating.* Leiden: E. J. Brill.

———. 1977. The nature of dynamic equivalence in translating. *Babel* 23, no. 3.

Oller, J. W., Jr. 1979. *Language tests at school.* New York: Longman.

Roberts, R. 1993. Student competencies in interpreting: Defining, teaching, and evaluation. In *Proceedings of the ninth national convention, Conference of Interpreter Trainers*, ed. E. A. Winston.

Schultz, J. M. 1991. Mapping and cognitive development in the teaching of foreign language writing. *The French Review* 64, no. 6 (May): 978–88.

Seleskovitch, D. 1978. *Interpreting for international conferences: Problems of language and communication.* Washington, D.C.: Pen and Booth.

Voice-to-sign interpreting practice: Living fully. 1994. Produced by Sign Enhancers, Salem, Ore. Videocassette.

Appendix 1

Buying My Condo by Clayton Valli

This tape was produced with funds from the U.S. Department of Education in a grant awarded to the Department of Linguistics and Interpreting at Gallaudet University. The grant is entitled "Interpreter Training for Deaf Individuals." The transcription is taken from the voice interpretation provided with the text.

Not too long ago I purchased a condo, which I had no intention of doing; I surprised myself, and I'm going to tell you about how the purchase came about.

I've been living in the D.C. metro area for the past ten years and during that time I've seen a lot of residences: houses, townhouses, condos. I've talked to some of my friends about their own purchases and just kind of gotten a feel for the market, what's out there, what houses, you know, different kinds of residences are selling for these days and just kind of checked out the whole market.

And during my travels around town I've gone to some open houses, just to get an idea, and I was on one particular street that I was really taken by. And I didn't know if there was ever going to be anything for sale on this street that I could afford, or if anything would ever come out of it. But this particular street stuck in my mind after I left the area.

So I continued my window shopping or just attending open houses for the enjoyment of it, to get an idea of the D.C. area, and perhaps find a location that I would be interested in settling down someday. And I also would peruse the newspapers and see what was out there. One day I noticed a condo for sale that was in the price range that I could afford, and I thought, you never know; take a look at it and let's see.

So I drove over to the address listed in the paper. When I got there I realized it was that street that I had been at some time before; it was the street that always stuck in my mind. So that was the first clue. And then when I went into the condo and looked around, it was a nice condo; I really liked it. So it started looking more and more like a real possibility.

So I talked to the real estate agent and asked him, "Well, you know, what's the actual price that this condo is selling for?" And he told me what the price was—he or she—and I said, "Well, you know, I could pay it but it's a little more than what I wanted to pay." I said, "Would you ask the owner if they would be willing to take ten thousand off the price?" The real estate agent didn't think that was very likely a possibility but said that they would give it a shot.

So I waited to hear back from the real estate agent, and finally they got back to me. And sure enough, the owners said they would be willing to take ten thousand off the price. I couldn't believe it! So, then I had to take a breath and think, well, this looks like this is really going to go. And not only that, interest rates were incredibly low—they were only 7 percent. And you know for quite a while now interest rates have been over 10 percent—11, even 12 percent. And I didn't know, you know, where am I going to find a deal like this again? They took ten thousand off the price, the interest rates are incredibly low, I don't know if I can pass this up. But, the only thing is at the same time I was also in school studying for my doctor's. So I really wasn't prepared to do this, but I decided I can't pass this up. So I said I'm just going to go ahead and do it.

So once I made the big decision, then I'd have to deal with the bank. So I got in touch with the bank, and they did an appraisal on the house and passed appraisal, and then they had to do a credit check, which I could not believe—down to the very penny these people checked my credit from the past two, three years. They went through all my credit cards, my bills, everything.

So I was going through the credit process, and everything was done, everything had passed. I was all set to go except for my car loan. The bank said I had 5 months left on my car loan, and I had to pay the whole thing off in one lump sum. So I added up what is 5 months of car payments, and it was a pretty big sum. And I didn't have that kind of money. So I got a hold of my mom and my sister, and my whole family helped out. And I still didn't have enough. I couldn't believe that the real estate agent actually chipped in and even helped me make that payment. So I was able to pay off my car loan.

So I got that taken care of, paid off my car, and everything was all set. The only thing was the owner still lived in the condo, so I had to wait for the owner to move out, which seemed to take forever. Finally, two months later after the initial viewing, to the day I moved in it was two months, and my friends were great—they helped me take all my furniture over there and got me all moved in and settled and everything so I could get back to studies on my Ph.D. I moved in and had my condo, and I'm all through with my studies. It's all done.

APPENDIX 2

Transcription of *Living Fully*

(This transcription was made from the spoken text.)

1. Welcome to what I hope will be an opportunity for personal growth to all who join me today.
2. My name is Jenna Cassell
3. and in my life I've assumed several different titles and numerous roles,
4. but today I simply wish to share with you some exciting ideas in order to help us all to grow.
5. For when we open ourselves to growth at a personal level, we enhance our ability to more fully experience our lives.
6. These ideas come from many rich sources;
7. however, the main resources used to formulate this presentation,
8. which I highly recommend,
9. include an audio program entitled "Freedom from Fear," by Reverend Mary Boggs of the Living Enrichment Institute,
10. A book entitled *Feel the Fear and Do It Anyway* by Susan Jeffers,
11. *Life Is an Attitude* by Elwood N. Chapman,
12. and finally *Peace, Love, and Healing* by Dr. Bernie S. Siegel.
13. I'd like to begin by telling you a story.
14. There once were three brickmasons working together on a building.
15. A little boy happened by
16. and asked the first brickmason, What are you doing?
17. Without even looking up, he responded,
18. I'm laying bricks!
19. The little boy approached the second (index front right) brickmason
20. and asked him,
21. What are you doing?
22. The second brickmason looked kindly at the boy and said,
23. I'm building a wall.
24. The little boy approached the third brickmason
25. and asked the same question.
26. What are you doing?
27. The brickmason faced him squarely and replied with enthusiasm (body shifting during role play) and obvious pride,
28. I am building a beautiful cathedral.
29. Now, if this little boy approached you and asked you,
30. What are you doing?

31. How would you respond?
32. Do you feel as though you simply lay bricks,
33. or do you retain the original joy and enthusiasm of your life choices?
34. Do you simply go through your routine in an unconscious manner
35. or do you always keep in the forefront of your mind (point to head) a vision of your beautiful cathedral?
36. Our minds are very powerful tools.
37. How we experience our life's work,
38. and indeed our lives,
39. is to a great degree a function of what we tell ourselves.
40. You see, the man laying bricks performs the very same task as the man who was building a beautiful cathedral,
41. but his inner experience was quite different.
42. We do have the power to affect our own perspective
43. and therefore our internal experience of external events.
44. We've all heard about positive self-talk,
45. that what you tell your self is very likely to become your reality.
46. Well, if this is true,
47. how do we turn our negative self-chatter into powerful "I can" messages?
48. Well, one thing to understand is that the brain tries to find answers to the questions posed to it.
49. So, if you could ask yourself questions that will elicit a positive response,
50. you have a head start on seeing the world in a positive way.
51. For example, when you first wake up in the morning,
52. do you ask yourself questions like this:
53. What do I have to do today?
54. What problems am I gonna have ta face? (voice inflection)
55. What's gonna happen if I fail at the challenges facing me?
56. Or try some of these questions instead?
57. What am I excited about today?
58. What challenges can I look forward to learning from today?
59. What new opportunities can I create today?
60. When facing a new challenge,
61. or what some people call a problem,
62. what kind of questions do you ask yourself?
63. Do you ask,
64. What could I lose if I try and fail?
65. Or, how about this?
66. What could I lose if I don't try?

67. What could I gain by trying, whether I succeed or not?
68. Often, we're stuck in negativity or negative emotions,
69. such as anger, depression, anxiety, to name a few.
70. It's important to recognize that these negative emotions that we're experiencing
71. are actually based in fear.
72. Fear of failure,
73. fear of being hurt,
74. fear of being humiliated,
75. fear of not having enough money,
76. fear of being alone.
77. I'm sure you could add to the list.
78. For example, if you get angry because someone cuts you off when you're driving,
79. the first thing that actually occurred was that
80. you experienced a fear of having a collision.
81. The anger was actually based in fear,
82. as most negative emotions are.
83. Fear is the biggest inhibitor of us acting upon our dreams and living our lives fully.
84. We hold back from participating in life fully
85. because we are afraid.
86. We're afraid to speak our truth,
87. we're afraid to show up in the world as we are,
88. and we're holding back in some way because of our fears.
89. Well, sad to say, it's not possible to do away with fear completely.
90. Every person on this planet experiences fear.
91. We all have fear in our lives.
92. Think about it.
93. Where is fear controlling you right now?
94. We all have fear in our lives.
95. Even the people who are very successful and self-confident,
96. who are out there making their dreams a reality,
97. experience fear.
98. Therefore, fear is not the problem.
99. What we do with the fear is what determines how we live our lives.
100. Although we can't eliminate fear,
101. we can view it differently
102. and deal with it in healthy and productive ways.
103. You see, we each have places, events, situations with which we're comfortable.

104. This is known as our comfort zone.
105. We each have our very unique comfort zone
106. based on our own past experiences, our perceptions of our capabilities, and our willingness to be out in the world.
107. Some people are only comfortable in the confines of their own home.
108. Others venture out into the world into the workplace,
109. and others still seem to make the whole world their home.
110. But when a challenge is presented that is outside our personal comfort zone,
111. fear appears.
112. Sometimes our fear induces enough self-doubt
113. that it actually prevents us from moving ahead.
114. We allow the fear to immobilize us
115. and to stop us from living fully or realizing our dreams.
116. Well, what's the alternative?
117. If we could shift our perspective and see fear instead as an ally that is telling us,
118. proceed with caution, but proceed.
119. A warning, if you will,
120. that says clearly and boldly,
121. "Growth opportunity ahead."
122. So, when you felt the fear, you would know that you are actually moving in the right direction
123. toward growth, toward expanding your comfort zone, toward living fully.
124. If we can face our fears squarely and imagine in the safety of our minds,
125. which after all is where fear exists,
126. how we might deal with the challenge,
127. we could take steps toward experiencing the fear and moving forward.
128. We could make progressive approximations toward expanding our comfort zone.
129. You can begin by imagining the worst possible consequences.
130. What if the worst happened?
131. And imagine yourself handling it.
132. Every experience we've had began in thought and was projected into the world of being.
133. Thoughts with feeling become reality.
134. We must create what we do in this world twice.
135. Once in our minds

136. and then again out in the world to make it so.
137. So facing the fear and imagining
138. "how would you handle that situation?" (overlap of constructed dialogue and indirect)
139. makes it easier to proceed with optimism.
140. And, as Oscar Wilde said,
141. the basis of optimism is sheer terror.
142. But how can we get past our fears?
143. As Susan Jeffers says in her book of the same title,
144. feel the fear and do it anyway,
145. each time we venture beyond the confines of our comfort zone,
146. we discover new ways of being.
147. We discover inner strength and abilities.
148. We learn to expect bigger and better things from ourselves.
149. Expectation is another very powerful determiner of events.
150. I'd like to share a story with you about a young man who took the scholastic aptitude test,
151. the SAT,
152. as part of the college entrance procedures.
153. When he received his test scores, he saw the number 98 on the paper.
154. Well, he was quite distressed and concerned about his ability to succeed in college with an IQ as low as 98.
155. But he did go to college.
156. His first term he received Ds and Fs.
157. His second term was no better,
158. and the dean called him in for a conference.
159. The dean warned him that if his performance continued at this poor level,
160. he would be asked to leave the school.
161. "Well, whaddo you expect?" replied the young man?
162. "I only have an IQ of 98."
163. The dean took out the file and explained to the young man,
164. "You don't have an IQ of 98;
165. you scored in the 98th percentile.
166. That means that your score was equal to or better than 98 percent of the students in all of North America."
167. Well, the next term, that student pulled a 4.0 grade point average.
168. The only thing that had changed was his expectations.
169. Another example of how powerful expectations are in determining events
170. was shown in a research project conducted in San Francisco.

171. Three teachers had been brought into the principal's office and told,
172. "You three teachers are the best teachers in this whole school.
173. We have decided to reward your performance by giving you each thirty of the best students."
174. These teachers were asked,
175. "Don't tell any of the students or the parents about this."
176. At the end of the year, it was found that these students tested significantly higher than all of the students,
177. not only in the school,
178. but in the entire district.
179. The teachers were brought in again.
180. They were informed that this had been an experiment
181. and that the students had actually been selected at random.
182. Well, the teachers were amazed,
183. and they could explain the high scores only by the fact that, they were, after all, the best teachers.
184. Well, then the researchers informed them,
185. "Actually, we put all the teachers' names in a hat,
186. and yours were the three that were pulled.
187. This was a double blind study
188. with the only factor not being controlled for being expectation.
189. In summary, if we learn to live with fear as an ally
190. which navigates our path in the direction of growth,
191. use our minds and strength of spirit to expand our personal comfort zone,
192. and learn to expect bigger and better things of ourselves,
193. we will enhance our ability to live more fully with a constant focus on our beautiful cathedrals.
194. I'd like to leave you with a poem that says,
195. Come to the edge, he said,
196. No, they replied, we will fall.
197. Come to the edge, he said.
198. No, we will fall.
199. Come to the edge.
200. They went to the edge
201. He pushed them, and they . . . flew.
202. I wish you all a good flight.
203. Thank you.

KYRA POLLITT

Critical Linguistic and Cultural Awareness

Essential Tools in the Interpreter's Kit Bag

WE ARE IN the business of making judgments about people. It is an activity that we indulge in every day of our working lives. Some will try to claim that they do not judge people, others will punish themselves for making such judgments. But let's face it, it is part of the job—how else is one to reflect the speaker and determine speaker intent? [1]

As with all areas of applied linguistics, interpreting struggles at the interface between art and science. We are aware that what we practice is a skill, some would say an art, but we need to be able to define, justify, and teach that skill in a logical, consistent, and rigorous manner. For example, how is it that good interpreters seem instinctively able to make the *right* judgments? How can we make good interpreters aware of and in control of what they do and teach student interpreters to do it, too?

I'd like to thank all the 1996–1997 and 1997–1998 City Lit interpreting course participants as well as the course coordinator Jemina Napier for their hard work and enthusiasm. In addition, I'd like to thank Norman Fairclough for his wise tuition and kind encouragement, Graham Turner for his love, support, and childcare, and Jacob and Edie for their patience while Mummy worked.

1. *Speaker* refers here to an active interactant, regardless of the mode of communication. Hence *speaker* may equally refer to someone who is using a signed language to communicate.

CULTURE AND INTERPRETING

The way some programs teach "culture" does not help. Many, particularly the increasing number of interpreting candidates coming through "hothouse" training programs,[2] may be exposed to only the superficial elements of Deaf culture,[3] and may not be encouraged to reflect on the wider culture at all. Being encouraged to think *this person belongs to that cultural group and therefore must hold the values x, y, and z* does little to refine one's ability to appreciate a person's Weltanschauung[4] (a person's worldview). Understanding the D/deaf communities' wider relations to the speaking world, then, may be more important to a practicing interpreter than spending hours debating the more superficial symbols of Deaf culture, such as how Deaf people attract each other's attention. It is the peculiar reality of Deaf people in relation to the dominant (oral-aural) world order that makes interpreting so interesting and difficult. Deaf people do not simply constitute a linguistic minority, but their signed languages encode and represent a minority way of being, of perceiving the natural world—and hence the dominant social order.

Perceptions of Interpreting

Perceptions of interpreting affect our understanding of an interpreter's role in interpreted events. Interpreters are often trained to believe that they are "invisible," that they have (or should have) little or no impact on the communication and the interaction that is taking place around and through them. Anyone who has ever had their

---

2. *Hothouse* is a term used to describe short, intensive interpreter training courses designed to offer a quick-fix solution to the shortage of interpreters. Students of these courses are likened to flowers intensively cultivated in hothouses.

3. The use of capital D in "Deaf" follows a convention established by James Woodward (1972) to distinguish those people for whom deafness constitutes a shared (signed) language, culture, and ethnicity from "deaf" people, who have a hearing loss but would lay no claim to the Deaf culture.

4. *Weltanschauung* is a German word, indicating the totality of one's experiences and perspectives in life; it is widely used in European literature on interpreting and translating (for example, see Nord 1997).

own communication interpreted will recognize the patent nonsense of this claim. As interpreters, we too are products of the societies in which we live/have lived. We have our own Weltanschauungs that inform and affect everything we do—including interpreting.

And what of ethics? Most extant codes of ethics deny the interpreter's impact on events and are only really effective tools in the hands of experienced practitioners. Trainees are often encouraged to learn these codes verbatim, as if that were sufficient to instill in them a critical sensitivity.

Training programs often teach important areas of interpreting, such as speaker intent, interpreter role, ethics, and others in less than satisfactory ways not because they are inferior courses but because these areas are so complex that it has been difficult to navigate a clear course through them. I believe that Critical Discourse Analysis (CDA) provides us with at least a compass.

CRITICAL DISCOURSE ANALYSIS

I first encountered CDA as an MA student in the linguistics department at Lancaster University. I was immediately struck by how relevant it was to my daily life as an interpreter. By lucky coincidence I was offered the chance to train two enthusiastic groups of students at the City Literary Institute in London, from 1996 to 1998. I seized the opportunity to experiment with my new-found theories and was delighted to discover that the course participants not only furthered my thinking considerably but they actively enjoyed the process (or so they said!). The twelve students in each course had had some experience in the field and were currently working as trainee interpreters, but they had had limited access to training. This chapter presents a portion of a course that ran for several months. I hope that you and your students will find it as interesting and stimulating as I did and feel sure that you will generate many new classroom activities of your own from this material.

Critical Discourse Analysis (CDA) differs from other types of discourse analysis in a number of significant ways. First, drawing on the philosophical works of Habermas, Lyotard, Heidegger, Foucault, and Derrida, we can place it fairly and squarely in the postmodernist stable. Consequently, its central tenet is the notion that there is no *grand recit*, no one culture to which we may lay claim, but that individuals have their own *petits recits*, their own particular blend of influences, ideas, ways of using language, and so on. In addition, CDA sees discourse (the way we talk about what we talk about) as an act of identity, as social action. It should be possible, therefore, to pick apart what we say and the way we say it to reveal some of the influences and beliefs that shape our lives, frame our perspectives, and characterize our speech.

That is the classroom activity that I will introduce here. For a full account of critical discourse analysis, see the work of Norman Fairclough (particularly Fairclough 1992, 225–41). The particular classroom activity that I describe helps interpreters define, analyze, control, and justify some of their judgments about interactants and their communications. This practice led to a reexamination of the interpreter's role (as discourse mediator) and to deeper discussions of ethical issues (where the boundaries of discourse mediating end and moral intervention begins). We found that the application of CDA to the interpreting task gave us a more satisfactory framework for these discussions. Unfortunately, it is beyond the scope of this chapter to detail the work we did on role and ethical issues; trainers, however, should be aware that this work will affect these areas (see the list of further reading in Appendix 1).

Step One: Theoretical Background

The first step for the trainer is to ensure that students have grasped the theoretical background of the work. The aim is to rid students of rigid, monolithic notions of culture and replace them with a more postmodern, eclectic vision. To this end I find the work of Habermas particularly useful. Habermas (1987) argues that most cultures form their own "lifeworlds" that interact with the broader "public sphere" in the manner illustrated in Figure 1.

In an earlier exercise, I encouraged the students to consider the position of the British Deaf community in relation to Habermas's

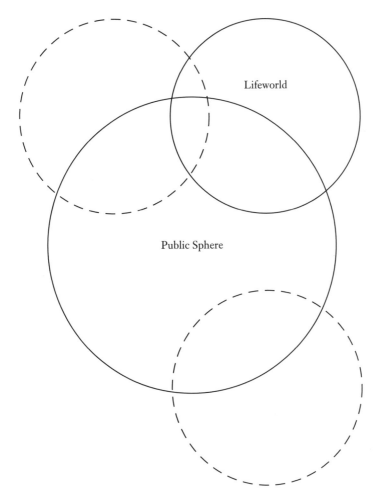

Figure 1. The Intersection of Lifeworlds and the Public Sphere

model. What we produced can be seen in Figure 2, which describes how Deaf people can access aspects of the public sphere (or English-speaking sphere) only by negotiating a simultaneously familiar and alien (English-speaking) lifeworld.

The work of Brian Street (1991) encourages us to think of culture as a verb, introducing the notion that we might "culture" ourselves differently at different times, in different places, and with different

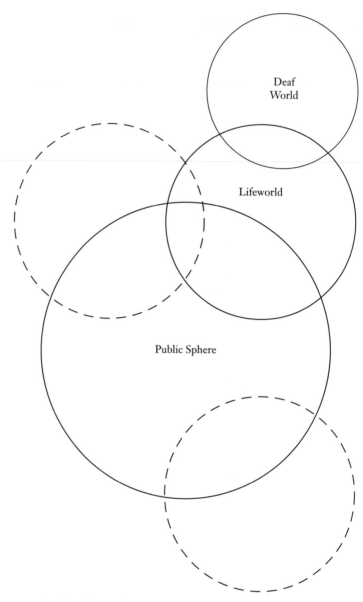

Figure 2. Deaf People's Access to the Public Sphere

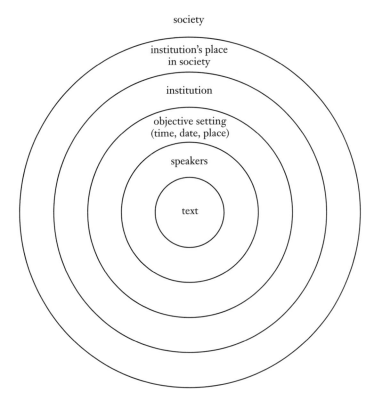

Figure 3. The Influence of Discourse on Identity. Adapted from Wodak, *Disorders of Discourse.*

people (that we might choose to hop in and out of any given life-world on a whim). The graphic shown in Figure 3, taken from Ruth Wodak's (1996) work, illustrates that our identities as speakers/signers are heavily influenced by the discourses to which we are exposed throughout our lives.

Wodak asserts that individuals are shaped, and their communications are *framed*, by the discourses present in their society, in the institutions to which they owe allegiance, and so on. Indeed, CDA theorists suggest that, without placing discourse in a broader context of social relations, we cannot hope to comprehend the full meaning of the message and the speaker's intent. Once students have grasped these fundamentals, it is time to move on to the next step—undertaking analysis. To help students focus on the aims of analysis, it is useful to keep the illustrations in Figures 1–3 on display in the classroom.

Step Two: Preparing for Analysis

Analysis should not be undertaken once. Rather like the hours of poetry and literary criticism that students of English are expected to undertake, CDA is a practice, not an exercise. This practice is repeated time and time again, with the aim of heightening students' critical language and cultural awareness and reflexes.

I recommend that students work either as a whole group or in groups of no less than four. The opportunity to share perspectives and have one's assumptions challenged is vital. Where this is not possible, the instructor must be prepared to work intensively with individual students, insisting that each student justify every assumption. It is important to be selective about the texts. Initially I would recommend texts that are synthesized from experience. Such synthesized texts lack the complexity of natural texts and so are useful in the earlier stages when students might be grappling with technique. Later it is possible to progress to more complex natural texts. As students gain experience, one *might* introduce texts taken from magazines, newspapers, and television talk shows (CDA does not suffer the same strictures of source material as other discourse analysis practices). Here, however, students should be encouraged to recognize the effect on the text of the standard formatting of magazine, television, or other types of media.

I recommend beginning with a monologue in the students' first language (L1). Present the text (which may take the form of an audiotape, written transcription, video excerpt, and so on) and ask students what they think the text means and what they know about the speaker of the text. It is important to give as little guidance as possible at this stage in order to elicit the widest range of comments (rather like matched guise testing) (Lambert 1967). Ask students to note the attributes they assigned to the speaker. From the following sample written text, my students' speculations included factors such as the speaker's profession, education, height, and even attractiveness!

Sample Text 1

The class was told that this text was taken from a Deaf woman meeting with a local education authority to discuss placing the woman's Deaf daughter in a local school. An interpreter is present.

> Hello, come in. Nice to meet you. I understand that you wish to talk to me about your daughter's schooling. Now she's hearing impaired, too, isn't she? And she's currently at Cherry Tree Juniors, and you want her to be transferred to the old Deaf and Dumb school? Actually, you know, my great aunt was hard of hearing, and I learned some of the sign language myself when I was in the Brownies. Of course, that's quite a few years ago now, but I still remember a bit of it. . . . That's A, isn't it? Yes, very good. Can you lipread me all right?

At first, students assess the education official as ill tempered and unprofessional. When students are shown how to undertake a more detailed structural analysis of the same text, they reexamine it, looking for evidence of the discourse of officialdom, women's discourse, the discourse of motherhood, and so on. At the conclusion of the analysis, students have changed their opinion about the education official; she is now perceived as an older professional who lacks modern Deaf awareness but who was making an effort to bring her experiences and resources to bear on this situation. It became obvious to the group that as interpreters, their original assessments of the official's intent would have greatly affected their interpretation, perhaps leading to conflict. After analysis, however, their interpretation would reflect the official's good intentions along with her lack of information, potentially leading to a different outcome.

Step Three: More Complex Analysis

As students undertake more detailed and structural analysis of texts, they are looking for features of discourse such as topic range, foregrounding and backgrounding of information, turn taking/ interrupting strategies, hedging, pausing, terms of address/relational markers, register shifts, prosody and intonation/nonmanual features, lexical choices, gender markers, the use of interrogatives versus declaratives, modals, the use of definite versus indefinite articles, and so on. These features should help students to identify discourses, justify such observations with reference to specific linguistic features, and predict areas of possible cultural conflict.

In this way students begin to piece together an understanding of the speaker that is based on something more tangible than gut instinct. It is instructive and enlightening to compare students' postanalysis findings with their initial opinions. As students become more familiar with the practice, you can move on to more complex natural texts, including dialogues, and eventually to "manufactured" texts (i.e., those taken from magazines, television programs, etc.).

After the class has worked through all levels of texts in L1, move on to texts in L2, again starting with simple, synthesized monologues. When the students have become proficient at analyzing complex L2 texts, proceed to bilingual texts. Eventually the students can work with bilingual texts, which they then interpret, comparing analysis of the original bilingual text with analysis of their own interpretations.

The following is an example of a more complex, "manufactured" text with an example of its analysis. The text is taken from a British Broadcasting Corporation (BBC) news report (broadcast in 1996) on cochlear implantation.

Sample Text 2

This is a BBC TV news broadcast that begins with pictures of the Elkins, hearing parents of a deaf child, waiting by the bedside of their daughter who is about to be wheeled down a hospital corridor to an operating room where she will undergo surgery for a cochlear implant. A female reporter narrates over these images and talks with the parents. As the broadcast proceeds, we see a number of live unscripted interviews (called vox pops) with other families and their children. In the following excerpt the normal rules for transcriptions apply. Each period indicates a pause of up to 2 seconds, and signed communication is shown in italics.

Reporter: There's a growing division among deaf people about a surgical operation that can help mute children hear and speak . cochlear implants give children the chance to lead a more normal life but at the cost of losing the deaf culture of sign language . the British Deaf Association is calling for an independent review . cochlear implants were pioneered by surgeons in Nottingham where an appeal gets underway this month to develop a specialist family center .

Elkins Father: *it's broken* *hey hey*

Elkins Mother: *hey*

Reporter: Kristina Elkins may have been born

Elkins Father: *tell your mum*

Elkins Mother: *what color*

Reporter: profoundly deaf but soon thanks to life-transforming surgery she may be able to hear and

Elkins Mother: *K, what color what*

Reporter: eventually to speak

Elkins Mother: *color is it*

Reporter: it will involve a major operation on her brain. her parents believe they must seize the chance

Elkins Father: to hear her voice for the first time will just be . unbelievable but . the communication is so limited because we don't wanna go too far with the sign . er . it'll make our lives a lot easier and Kristina . erm . to be able to communicate with her brother Callum as well

Elkins Mother: it really is is . er . our only chance to actually get sound in and try and understand the world as . . . you know we see it and hear it and to be able to go on and do things as normal children in mainstream school'n . things like 'at

Reporter: Kristina is on her way now to have the operation which her parents hope will transform her life . what she can't know is that the type of operation she is about to have is the subject of fierce debate within the deaf community and there are many who believe she should not be having it at all . in fact doctors at the implant center in Nottingham believe the controversy is one reason why they are treating only two-thirds of the deaf children who could benefit . the implant works by stimulating the hearing nerve directly sounds are then interpreted by a processor worn outside the body . for the King family the operation has been little short of a miracle James became deaf after getting meningitis as a baby . he faces several years of training but already sign language is giving way to speech

King Mother: I can shout to him from the top of the stairs and he turns around and he can he knows where the sound is coming from he knows it's me and he's now beginning to put sentences together and we're sort of like we're picking up where we left off at sixteen months when he left er when he lost his hearing

Woman: *listen look   look*
Reporter: the younger the patient the better the results and that's the cause of disquiet among
    many deaf
Girl: *come and sit here come on*
King Mother: *wait !*
Reporter: people . the British Deaf Association is pressing for an independent inquiry into the
    whole process concerned that the child's best interests are not always put first.

Sample Analysis

Concessions to the discourse of deafhood (a discourse of language
rights and ethnicity) within the reporter's narrative occur through
the use of key words and phrases such as "deaf people" rather than
"the deaf," "deaf culture," "sign language," and "deaf community."
However, without exception, these elements are placed in oppositional, contrastive relationships with elements of medical discourse
within their governing sentences. The reporter's opening sentence
is a prime example:

> There's a growing division among deaf people about a surgical oper-
> ation that can help mute children hear and speak.

Here the adjective "deaf" contrasts with "mute," which serves
to medicalize both words and divorces the "children" from the
"people" who, in a deafhood discourse, would represent their heri-
tage community. Similarly the negatively framed activity of deaf
people—"division"—contrasts with the positively framed activity
of the surgical operation—"help." The addition of the verbs "hear"
and "speak," which are attributed to the "children" (the noun), shifts
the balance of the structural axis of the sentence in favor of the medical discourse elements.

Later in the text the reporter, when speaking about James, who
has already had the implant, says, "but already sign language is giving way to speech." In this sentence the verb phrase "giving way"
positions the noun "speech" as the stronger of the two noun phrases.
This pattern is repeated throughout the narration. Returning to the
beginning of the report, the reporter says:

> Cochlear implants give children the chance to lead a more normal life
> but at the cost of losing the deaf culture of sign language.

The noun phrase "cochlear implants" governs the verb phrase "give children the chance," which has a positive connotation, whereas the second noun phrase "deaf culture of sign language" is governed by the more negatively connotated phrase "cost of losing." The oppositional relationship is highlighted by the contrasting conjunction "but." We see this again with another sentence:

> Kristina Elkins may have been born profoundly deaf but soon thanks to life-transforming surgery she may be able to hear and eventually to speak.

This sentence is an excellent example of the conflation of the discourses of deafhood and disability. The adjectival phrase "profoundly deaf " occupies a position in the sentence thus far reserved for the element of deafhood discourse—that is, in opposition to the phrase "hear and eventually to speak." The adjective "profoundly" more properly belongs to disability discourse and has a negative effect because it is attached to "deaf." The narration constructs deafness as a biological condition from which individuals may be emancipated through the benefits of technology.

The first and most striking feature of the vox pops is their arrangement within the text as a whole. The medical discourse identified in the preceding paragraph frames the introduction to and exit from both video inserts. The texts of the two vox pops echo the narrative's theme of emancipation through normalcy. Although Kristina and her parents are first shown communicating manually, the spoken narration is overlaid, highlighting the relevant import given to each method of communication. Throughout the insert Kristina is never given a voice (either spoken or signed) as the audience is never allowed to witness her natural communication. The impression is thereby created of Kristina as being bereft of language. This is reinforced by the father's statement that "communication is so limited." Kristina's identity is backgrounded throughout with only one mention of her name and two pronouns that refer to her. When Kristina's mother talks about Kristina hearing and understanding the world, there is a curious omission of the object in her phrase "get sound in" (her ears?) as well as an omission of the subject in the next phrase (for her to?) "try and understand the world." The implication is that Kristina has no identity because identity can be defined only through oral/aural language.

In the second vox pop, James, who has already undergone surgery, is afforded an identity—an exclusively hearing/speaking one. Although his mother does not maintain that James is able to communicate exclusively orally/aurally, the report does not include footage of James signing, suggesting again that only speaking and hearing are the goal.

The use of vox pops as a textual device is evidence of what Fairclough (1995, 13) calls "conversationalization," or the conscription of features found in natural conversation to serve in "manufactured" texts. One may argue that such conversationalization serves to "naturalise the terms in which reality is represented" (Fowler in Fairclough, 1995, 13).

CONCLUSIONS

The students with whom I worked found the CDA activity engaging. In feedback, they reported the following:

1. increased overall language awareness
2. increased sensitivity to the perspectives of others
3. broadened perspectives
4. an increased appetite for knowledge of other cultural/belief systems
5. heightened self-awareness
6. a greater understanding of how such perspectives can affect the interpreted event.

REFERENCES

Fairclough, N. 1992. *Discourse and social change*. Oxford: Polity Press in association with Blackwell.
———. 1995. *Critical discourse analysis: The critical study of language*. London: Longman.

Habermas, J. 1987. *Theory of communicative action.* Vol. II: *Critique of functionalist reason.* Cambridge: Polity Press.

Lambert, W. 1967. A social psychology of bilingualism. *Journal of Social Issues* 23 (2): 91–109.

Nord, C. 1997. *Translating as a purposeful activity: Functionalist approaches explained.* Manchester: St. Jerome Publishing.

Street, B. 1991. Culture as a verb. Paper presented at the British Association of Applied Linguistics annual conference, University of Durham, Durham, U.K.

Wodak, R. 1996. *Disorders of discourse.* London: Longman.

Woodward, J. 1972. Implications for sociolinguistic research among the deaf. *Sign Language Studies* 1:1–7.

APPENDIX 1

Additional Reading

Fairclough, N. 1989. *Language and power.* London and New York: Longman.

Pollitt, K. 1998. Deconstructing Deafness: A critical discourse analysis of a BBC Breakfast News broadcast. Paper presented at Sociolinguistics Symposium 12, London.

———. 1998. Postmodernism and the death of the ethic? Paper presented at the International Internet Conference on Professional Practice, Boston, Mass.

Tate, G., and G. Turner. 1997. The code and the culture: Sign language interpreters in search of the new breed's ethics. *Deaf Worlds* 13 (3): 27–34.

Wodak, R. 1989. *Language, power, and ideology.* London: Longman.

MELANIE METZGER

Interactive Role-Plays
As a Teaching Strategy

STUDENTS OF INTERPRETATION are often taught that the inter-preter's role in interactive settings is that of a neutral service provider. This is likely due to the fact that interpreters have long been viewed as merely a tool to interaction. For example, the tradi-tional view assumes that interactive discourse facilitated by an inter-preter is a dyad between two monolinguals or between deaf and hearing participants rather than a triad that includes the interpreter as a participant. In conjunction with this view, the field of inter-preting has perpetuated the expectation that interpreters will not be involved in interpreted interactions. Evidence for this exists in the sign language interpreters' professional Code of Ethics by the Reg-istry of Interpreters for the Deaf, Inc. (RID) in the United States. The third tenet of the code states:

> An interpreter . . . shall not become personally involved because in
> so doing he/she accepts some responsibility for the outcome, which
> does not rightly belong to the interpreter. (Frishberg 1990, 197)

Yet, recent research calls into question the assumption that it is pos-sible for an interpreter to function as a passive conduit. For example, interpreters have been found to take an active role in the turn ex-changes in interpreted encounters (Roy 1989, 1993) and to contrib-ute self-generated utterances that not only relay the utterances of the primary participants but also fulfill a coordinating function, at

83

times providing information that no one has uttered but which is
nonetheless an inherent part of the interaction, such as the identity
of the original source (Wadensjö 1992; Metzger 1995, 1999). In addition, Zimmer (1989) discusses ways in which interpretation, via
features such as lengthy pauses, influences the participants' behavior and possibly even their perception of one another. These findings raise questions both about how interpreters influence or
participate in interpreted interaction and how this issue is addressed
in interpreter education.

Because interpreters have been found to take a more active role in
interactive settings, sometimes negotiating participants' turn taking, at other times asking for clarification or providing supplemen-
tary information (such as indicating the source of a given utterance),
the teaching of simultaneous interactive interpretation is not simply
an extension of monologic interpreting skills. Students who have already studied and mastered interpreting monologic discourse from
a source language to a target language will have knowledge and skills
related to comprehension, finding equivalence, and production of
the target text. Additional skills that these students must learn in order to develop interactive interpreting expertise are (1) the ability to
switch back and forth between languages rapidly, (2) knowledge of
the features of interaction (such as overlap), and (3) the ability to appropriately generate relevant contributions to the interaction (such
as indicating the source of an utterance).

Although videotapes are often used to teach and evaluate interactive interpreting skills, they do not realistically capture conversational turn taking and overlap or many other features of interactive
discourse that practicing interpreters face on a daily basis. Thus, one
of the most important tools that interpreter educators have for
teaching interactive interpreting skills is the role-play. Role-plays
can be more or less meaningful for interpreting students depending
on the extent to which the students' metalinguistic knowledge about
interaction is utilized by the activity and the extent to which the
role-play realistically captures the features of natural interactions
that interpreting students will eventually face in the professional
arena (Metzger 1995, 1999).

INTERACTIVE ROLE-PLAYS AS A TEACHING STRATEGY

When selecting the role-play as a strategy for teaching interactive interpretation, three objectives should guide the interpreter educator. These three objectives surpass the goals established for any interpretation (e.g., simultaneous monologic) related to equivalence and language production. That is, while the interpreter educator will certainly provide feedback to the students regarding the equivalence of their translations and their choice and production of words and sentences in the target utterances, the three primary objectives of the interactive role-play are for students to be able to do the following:

1. Recognize and identify features of interactive discourse
2. Understand interpreters' strategies for coping with interactive discourse
3. Apply strategies for coping with interactive discourse

These three objectives provide a simple guide for distinguishing between the interpretation of monologic and dialogic or multiparty discourse.

Objective #1: Recognize and Identify Features of Interactive Discourse

Objective #1 refers to the process of taking linguistic knowledge that students already have as native users of a language and making students more aware of that knowledge so that they can apply it to the interpreting task. Although the features found in interactive discourse might be common across languages (for example, most language communities have rules governing conversational turn taking), the specific details about how the features are manifested linguistically may differ among languages. An example of this can be seen in the turn-taking feature of interaction. Sacks, Schegloff, and Jefferson (1974) analyzed spoken English conversation and identified features of the point in a conversation at which participants can (without interrupting) enter into a conversation and take a turn.

In English, the linguistic devices that signal appropriate moments to take the floor can relate to the pace, pauses, and pitch of the speaker's utterance, depending on the speakers and their conversational style (see Tannen 1984, 1986). In American Sign Language (ASL) the linguistic devices will obviously be quite different. Baker (1977) examined conversation regulators in ASL and found that a variety of manual and nonmanual signals are related to turn taking. For instance, when a signer directs eyegaze toward an addressee in conversation, that might signal to the addressee that she or he can attempt to take a turn. Whether in English, ASL, or any other language, linguistic signals such as these are unconsciously acquired by native users of the language. The purpose of the first objective is to assist interpreting students in gaining a metalinguistic awareness of the features of interactional discourse in their native language as well as in any other languages with which they will be working as interpreters (see Appendix 1 for a list of recommended readings related to Objective 1).

Although gaining a more conscious awareness of interactional discourse is very useful to interpreting students, it is not enough to simply understand these discourse features in each language. This is very apparent in interpreted phone conversations, which can often be full of awkward pauses and overlapping turns that challenge the interpreter. When an interpreter interprets between a spoken language and a signed language, such as English and ASL, participants can easily misgauge or misunderstand when it is appropriate to attempt to take a turn in the conversation because the linguistic signals are not even based in the same mode. Thus, an interpreter is likely to encounter professional situations in which both participants attempt to take a turn at the same time, and the interpreter must be prepared to handle that situation appropriately (see Roy 1989, 1993). Interactive discourse is affected by the presence of an interpreter, and this is the rationale for Objective #2.

Objective #2: Understand Interpreters' Strategies for Coping with Interactive Discourse

Interpreters' strategies for coping with interactive discourse can be divided into two types (Wadensjö 1992; Metzger 1995, 1999): those related to the management of the interaction and those related to relaying the utterances made by participants. Research related to ASL–English interpretation has provided the following list of features related to interactional management:

1. Introductions
2. Summonses/attention-getting strategies
3. Turn taking and overlap
4. Responses to questions

Features related to relayings include the following:

1. Source attribution
2. Requests for clarification
3. Relaying of pronominal reference

A brief description of these features and how they have been observed to occur in ASL–English interpretation is provided in the following section. For a more in-depth discussion, see Roy (1989, 1993) and Metzger (1995, 1999).

Interactional Management

INTRODUCTIONS. Introductions are a common feature of many interactions. When friends or colleagues gather for business or social purposes, one of the first features one finds in their discourse is a round of introductions to make sure that all the interactants know one another. Depending on the language community and the purpose of the interaction, introductions might include only the name of an individual participant, or it might include background information such as the name of the school the participant attended or information about the participant's employment. When an interpreter will be working in any interactive setting, it is most likely to be both natural and beneficial for an introduction to be made, at least to introduce the interpreter as an interpreter and possibly to include additional information about the interpreter's role.

Introducing an interpreter seems a simple enough task. However, because at least two participants are not likely to have access to at least one of the languages and/or modes being used, a question arises regarding who should do the introductions and in what language or languages they should be conducted. If one or another participant introduces the interpreter, two potential problems result: (1) The introduction could include incorrect information about the interpreter or the interpreting process, and (2) A naive consumer could be confused about who is initiating the introduction because they do not yet have a schema for the operation of the interpreting process. If the interpreter conducts the introduction, then it must be done one language at a time (simultaneous signed-spoken introductions can be problematic; see Metzger 1995, 1999). Thus, the potential exists for one participant to feel excluded or of secondary importance. This is a significant consideration in many settings because it can have an impact on the quality of service being received by one of the participants.

These are just a few of the issues commonly faced by interpreters when coping with introductions. Although recent research provides some empirically based insight into these issues, more research remains to be done to offer clear-cut solutions. Thus, these are issues that should be discussed with students so that they are prepared to make decisions that are most likely to facilitate the interaction in whatever settings they find themselves working.

SUMMONSES. In spoken language interaction, participants who are in the same room know that simply through the act of producing an utterance they have access to one another linguistically. Participants might use a variety of attention-getting devices to summon one particular participant over another or for a variety of other reasons (see Goffman 1981). However, in signed language interaction among deaf participants, the same assumption cannot be made. Participants must get each other's visual attention in order to know that their utterances are being received. Such attention-getting devices can include hand waving, tapping the other participant, and moving the signed utterance to the level of, and in alignment with, the eyegaze of the other participant (for a discussion of eyegaze, see Mather 1994).

Although this concept should not be new to students of ASL–English interpretation, they should recognize that the hearing participants in an interpreted interaction will most likely not be aware of the need to visually summon the attention of a deaf participant. Thus, despite the fact that the hearing participant does not utter an English attention-getting utterance (such as calling the person's name), the interpreter might still be obliged to use one of the aforementioned strategies to ensure that the deaf participants know they are being addressed.

TURN TAKING AND OVERLAP. As discussed earlier, turn-taking regulators can differ among languages. Thus, two or more participants may find it difficult to know when to start and stop turns within an interpreted interaction. One result of this is that participants' utterances commonly overlap with one another, making it difficult (if not impossible) for the interpreter to relay both participants' utterances. The task of managing the turn-taking exchange in interpreted interaction falls to the one person who knows and uses both languages: the interpreter. This is true even if the interpreter's decision is to not regulate turns but rather to allow participants to try to work things out for themselves.

According to Roy (1989, 180–81), several options are available to interpreters when participants' utterances overlap, including:

1. Stopping one or both speakers;
2. Continuing to relay one person's utterance, remembering the second person's utterance and relaying it after the first has been completed;
3. Disregarding the overlap; and
4. Continuing to relay one person's utterance and, when done, offer a turn to the other participant (or otherwise indicate the attempted turn).

To make a professionally appropriate decision, the interpreting student must learn both how to accomplish each of these four options (e.g., what are appropriate ways to stop a speaker or signer, and how one listens to and interprets one utterance while also remembering another) and how to cope with the variety of possible responses. For example, a medical doctor might be less accustomed to being stopped in midturn than is a mental health counselor and might have a different reaction to option #1. Overlap is just one feature related to the turn-taking aspect of interactional management. For a more in-depth discussion, see Roy (1989).

RESPONSES TO QUESTIONS. During the course of an interpreted interaction, participants routinely direct questions to the interpreter. These questions can be related to the interaction itself, such as a request for clarification of something that the interpreter just said, or they can be less directly related but serve a social purpose, perhaps asking the interpreter how long she or he has worked in the field. Interpreters can respond to such questions in at least three ways: (1) ignore the questions and not respond; (2) provide a minimal response, not necessarily answering the question; or (3) provide a lengthier explanation, either in response to the question itself or to explain the interpreter's role. These are not the only possible alternatives, but they demonstrate a range of options that have been found to have varying impacts on interpreted interaction (see Metzger [1995, 1999] for a more detailed discussion).

To examine the impact of these various interpreter responses on interaction, we should first recognize that question-answer sequences represent one form of adjacency pair (Schegloff 1972; Schegloff and Sacks 1973). An adjacency pair is a two-part sequence in interactive discourse, such as a greeting. The first part of an adjacency pair is uttered by one participant, subsequently opening a slot that is expected to be filled by the addressee. The lack of a response to the first part is unusual and marked.

Question-answer sequences represent another type of adjacency pair. Language users who utter a question expect some sort of response to serve as the second part of the pair. Thus, when interpreters ignore questions that are directed to them, they leave an empty slot in the interaction, which is noteworthy and often uncomfortable to the other participant. A minimal response, even one that does not answer the question, fills the expectation for a second part and therefore is less likely to cause interactional problems. Understanding the sociolinguistic expectations of participants who direct questions to interpreters can assist students in determining how to respond in various settings and how to assess the result of their choices on the ensuing interaction.

Relayings

SOURCE ATTRIBUTION. In the interpretation of any interaction that involves more than two people, consumers will likely not know the source of a particular utterance unless the interpreter makes that information explicit. In fact, because interpreters themselves must often generate utterances (to stop a speaker who has overlapped or to summon the attention of a participant), even in an interaction with two participants, the interpreter represents a third person capable of contributing to the discourse. Thus, in any interpreted encounter, consumers cannot be certain who is responsible for a particular utterance unless the interpreter attributes the source (either to herself or someone else). Strategies for attributing source include naming the source, using a pronoun, pointing, shifting body position, and changing intonation to represent the voices of different participants.

Students should know what options they have and have the opportunity to practice using them. Discussion regarding which strategies work best and when they are most or least necessary can be very useful.

REQUESTS FOR CLARIFICATION. Seleskovitch (1978) has said that an interpreter cannot interpret what she or he does not understand. No interpreter can always have all the background knowledge needed for every assignment. Even relatively small details, such as names of places in an area to which an interpreter has recently moved, can prove to be uninterpretable if not understood. Therefore, during the course of an interpreted encounter, an interpreter might need to request clarification from one or another participant in order to continue interpreting. This need can also result from environmental distractions. Whatever the cause, interpreting students must understand the importance of making such requests and must learn appropriate ways to make such requests in interactive settings.

PRONOMINAL REFERENCE. Interpreters generally render interpretations as if they were first-person utterances. That is, when one participant says, "I am happy to meet you," the interpreter will also use the equivalent of the first-person pronoun "I" in the target language. However, in practice, interpreters do not always use pronouns that match those of the source text (see Wadensjö 1992, Metzger 1995, 1999). Moreover, interpreters have been found to eliminate comments such as, "Tell him . . ." from source utterances. Elimination of such comments removes the opportunity for the other participants to request that they be addressed directly.

All of the features discussed in this section, whether related to interactional management or relaying, are salient to the interpretation of interaction and should be addressed in role-plays. Ideally, students would be made aware of them as features first; then they will be worked into role-plays to the extent possible. This application of the strategies on the job is the focus of Objective #3.

Objective #3: Apply Strategies for Coping with Interactive Discourse

In the previous section, a variety of interpreters' strategies for coping with interactive discourse were identified. The purpose of a role-play is for students to actually apply these strategies. The following components are requisite to the establishment of an effective ASL–English simultaneous interactive role-play:

1. Participants (deaf and hearing)
2. Topics familiar to the participants

3. Permission forms
4. Video camera and videotapes
5. Scheduling of role-play within the course

Participants and Topics

Although any two people can be asked to participate in a role-play, the purpose of the role-play is to create as realistic as possible an interaction within the safe, learning environment of the classroom. In the case of ASL–English interpretation, it is important that the deaf participants be fluent signers of ASL and that the English speakers be nonsigners. Because most deaf Americans have at least some experience working with interpreters, and the majority of hearing Americans do not, it can be useful to invite deaf participants who are experienced professionals to participate in the role-plays. Wherever possible, involving deaf lawyers, financial specialists, medical professionals, and so forth will allow for the selection of topics with which interpreters will commonly work. Students will gain the additional benefit of being exposed to terminology in what is most likely not their first language. Moreover, to the extent that these participants are willing to be involved in class discussions, they provide an excellent resource for discussion of experience and preferences regarding the features discussed in the previous section.

Finding hearing participants who have a real-world interest in the topic is most desirable. For example, a hearing nonsigner who is interested in learning about investments will ask better and more realistic questions of a financial advisor. An additional consideration is that of experience being in front of a group. When local theaters or drama students are available, some excellent opportunities to request specific discourse features is the result. For instance, an actor can be asked to frequently interrupt the other participant in order to provide the student with an opportunity to cope with overlap. The use of actors offers this benefit to the teacher. However, the natural quality of the interaction might be less than that with an interested party. Perhaps the ideal situation is one in which an actor who is also personally interested in the topic can be found to participate.

A final point about participants is that interactive interpretation does not always consist of two participants. Even in settings typically involving two, such as interviews and telephone conversations, the presence of additional people who might either get involved with the conversation or offer distractions is quite common. Thus, involving more than two participants in role-plays can also be a useful and more realistic experience for students. Whereas the interpretation of multiparty settings might be a more advanced activity, the less advanced students can and should be exposed to variations such as interpreting for parents with their children present. Such experiences raise a wealth of topics for discussion about whether to interpret the child's discourse, how to include it, and how to read the one-handed signs of a parent holding a child on his lap. One effective approach to making the role-play more realistic in this way is to schedule it at the site of one of the professional participants as opposed to meeting in the classroom environment. In this way, all the interruptions common to that environment can occur and provide for a much more realistic preparation for students. It also provides an excellent opportunity for community members to learn more about the interpreting process.

In this section, a case has been made for involving professionals from the community to come into the classroom to participate in role-plays. Although many professionals are quite willing to support interpreter education, it is advisable to seek funding sources or find alternate ways of compensating people for their time. Not only does this promote a good relationship between the interpreter education program, the field of interpretation, and the community, but it can also go a long way toward ensuring that busy people actually arrive on time and are ready to go to work. It is also important to recognize that many professionals do not have total control over their own schedules. Whether deaf or hearing, lawyers, medical professionals, financial experts, real estate agents, and so forth might have a last-minute emergency that requires their attention and prevents them from attending a scheduled role-play. Planning the role-play at their location can be one potential solution to this problem. Another solution is to arrange backup participants for each role-play so that the activity need not be cancelled in such an event.

Video Camera, Videotapes, and Permission Forms

To gain the most from the role-play experience, students will not only interpret an interaction and discuss it, they will also need to actually review the interaction on videotape, recognize and note salient interactional features of the discourse, and critically analyze how the interpreter handled them. This means that a video camera will be a necessary component of the role-play activity. The video camera should meet two important criteria. First and most important, it should be of high enough quality to be able to provide videotapes that students can use for detailed analysis. Ideally, the camera will be able to adjust for various lighting conditions. It is also important to use videotapes of reasonable quality. Second, the camera should be mobile. Because some of the best role-plays do not occur in the confines of a classroom or language lab, the video camera will be needed at alternate sites. The smaller the camera is, the less intrusive it will be in the uncontrolled nonclassroom setting (many offices are not designed to accommodate several students and video equipment). In addition, the more lightweight the camera, the easier it will be to transport. A tripod will also come in handy. Depending on the logistics of the role-play, instructors might want to have more than one camera and lights available. However, the more technical the setup, the less natural the interaction is likely to be (see Labov 1972 and the Observer's Paradox).

The need for videotaping warrants the use of permission forms, so that deaf and hearing members of the community will be comfortable participating in the role-play. A form can be tailored to the individual class but should include the name of the participant, date and description of the activity, and the purpose for which the videotape will be used (see Figure 1 for a sample permission form).

Scheduling Role-Play within the Course

Because the role-play itself, as Objective #3, is the application of knowledge gained in Objectives #1 and 2, the sequencing of the role-play within the course is already somewhat clear. Nevertheless, it is useful to take a look at the scheduling of the role-play within an interactive interpretation course as a whole, so that the greatest

I, _____ (name), hereby give permission for my conversation at _____ (location) on _____ (date) to be videotaped. I understand that this videotape will be used for educational purposes by students to analyze their interpreting work and that it will not be copied, distributed, shown outside the classroom, or used for any other purpose.

_____ _____
(signature)   (date)

Figure 1. Sample Permission Form

benefit for the study of interaction—and not simply interpretation—can be provided. As mentioned earlier in the chapter, the interactive interpretation course itself should follow the study and acquisition of monologic simultaneous interpretation skills (e.g., ASL-to-English and English-to-ASL).

THE NATURE OF INTERACTIVE INTERPRETATION

A logical sequence for studying the nature of interactive interpretation is to start with metalinguistic study, then interpretation of interactive videotapes, and finish with live interactive role-plays.

Metalinguistic Study

The metalinguistic study of interactive discourse features and interpreted interaction can consist of readings and discussion. Numerous activities can supplement this, including assignments requiring that students identify specific features, perhaps through observations of both noninterpreted and interpreted interaction. In addition, because so many features of interaction are rapid and brief in nature (greetings as adjacency pairs, for example), it is particularly useful to use videotapes for these types of observations (numerous comedy sketches provide a humorous look at features of interactive discourse; see for example, episodes of Seinfeld or comedy sketches by

John Cleese on "How to Irritate People"). Fewer videotapes of interpreters coping with interaction are available on videotape, although some segments can be found in the popular media (see, for example, episode #2 of "I Love Lucy: The Collector's Edition: Lucy Goes Cuban" for a scene in which Ricky has difficulty interpreting between his Cuban mother and American wife). Most likely, nothing will replace the valuable experience of observing working interpreters interpreting interaction for the sole purpose of analyzing their coping strategies (e.g., source attribution, discussed earlier).

Interpretation of Interactive Videotapes

After students have had the opportunity to increase their understanding and conscious awareness of both noninterpreted and interpreted interaction, they are ready to begin applying it. However, for their first attempts, both privacy and pace are important factors to control. Thus, the use of interactive videotapes is very beneficial. For ASL–English interpretation, such tapes are available commercially, such as the one-to-one interviews available from Sign Enhancers, Inc., and Sign Media, Inc.

A benefit of these videotapes is that students (with access to appropriate equipment) can interpret them alone and proceed at their own pace. Additionally, teachers can make recommendations for students based on the pace of the tape and individual student skills. Moreover, practice with such videotapes is excellent preparation for future professional assessment of interpreting skills because many assessments are conducted via video. A negative aspect is that many interactive features are absent from videotaped interactions. For example, it is difficult to simulate natural conversational overlap on such media. Thus, these videotapes provide an excellent intermediate tool for the teaching of interactive interpretation, allowing students to focus on a limited number of features as they begin to apply what they have been learning.

Students should be expected to analyze their work with the videotaped sources. These analyses should address as many of the interactive features as they can while also addressing the usual issues related to any interpretation, such as production and equivalence. Once the students have mastered basic interpreting interaction and switching back and forth between languages, they are ready to begin to interpret live interactive role-plays.

Interactive Role-Play

In order to prepare the most effective interactive role-play for interpreting students, advanced planning is required. Certain matters can be addressed ahead of time, and others can be handled on the day of the role-play before it begins. By involving students in various facets of the role-play process, the logistics of conducting a role-play with community professionals in as realistic a manner as possible can be enhanced. Finally, certain steps in the discussion process and in student analysis can increase the educational quality of the experience.

Advanced Planning

Determining in advance which topics and professionals are preferable for the class is an important part of advanced planning. There are numerous topics and settings that can be addressed, including medical, legal, mental health, sales, business, financial, computer, religious, theatrical, educational, telephone, and video (e.g., instructional videos) themes. Any of these topics or settings could be the focus of an entire course on interactive interpretation, in which students study features unique to the setting (for example, doctors have general scripts that they follow in a medical interview and a format that includes examination and postexam consultation/diagnosis; moreover, doctors have been found to use specific types of language that can enhance or detract from the medical interview with or without interpreters (see Metzger 1995 for a discussion of this). The topics to cover and the number of role-plays to conduct during a semester will vary depending on the backgrounds and interests of class participants and the number of students. For instance, if one class has ten students, ten live role-plays allow each student to have one opportunity to interpret. Computing the number of students in the

Role-Play Scheduling Form						
Date	Time	Name	Address	Phone #/email	SS#	Topic

Figure 2. Sample Role-Play Scheduling Form

class and the number of students who will participate in a single role-play is key to successful advanced planning.

Compiling a list of community members who are willing to participate, with their phone numbers, addresses, e-mail addresses, and social security numbers (if they will be paid) can be very useful (see Figure 2). In addition, details about location will be useful to gather ahead of time. For example, when role-plays happen in the classroom, directions and maps can be sent to the guest participants in advance. When later role-plays are conducted on sites in the community, directions should be requested and distributed to students ahead of time.

Another issue to be decided in advance is how to handle the portions of the role-play before and after the invited participants interact. Initial introductions, preconferencing with students, and discussions of the role-play at its conclusion are all part of the process that will need to be interpreted for the deaf and hearing participants. Who will handle that interpreting should be decided in advance. An interpreter could be hired for the task, in which case sufficient funds must be secured. It is also possible for the teacher to interpret these portions of the process, although that can be difficult to manage well when he or she has the additional responsibility of guiding the event. Another option is for students who are not expected to interpret for the day to interpret these portions of class. Again, this depends on the experience and skills of the students in the class. Of these options, hiring an interpreter is the most preferable because it allows the teacher and all the students to fully participate in the role-play process.

Involving the community at large, when handled in advance, can make role-plays effective. Remembering to have backup participants available will also be useful. When professionals cannot be found to participate in a particular area, local colleges can become a resource. Many other professional education programs use role-plays to prepare their students (medical, legal, mental health, etc.). Joining forces with such programs can benefit both the interpreting students and the students who will work in other fields and likely encounter interpreters at some point in their career.

Pre-Role-Play Setup

The pre-role-play setup includes essentially three parts. First, it is important to have a premeeting with participants to finalize the topic, answer any questions they might have, and explain the process of the role-play itself (see the following section). This is the time to let participants know if you want them to elicit particular features, for example, by encouraging them to interrupt one another regardless of whether the interpretation is complete if they choose to do so. Because this can violate what some view as rules of conversational politeness, depending on their conversational style, some participants will be better able to do this than others. As mentioned earlier, for this reason utilizing actors in at least some role-plays can be beneficial. This premeeting with participants need not take more than 10–15 minutes and can be conducted before class begins.

In addition to the premeeting with participants, the room itself, whether a classroom, language lab, or community site, will need to be prepared for the role-play and video camera. It is very useful to involve students in this process. Because part of the students' future work is likely to include coordinating interpreter schedules and arranging for logistical issues, students can take on the responsibility for arranging their schedules and setting up the camera, chairs, and so forth. If possible, the logistical setup can also be planned for the 10–15 minutes just before class begins, to reserve maximum time for the role-play and discussion.

During the role-play, students should be engaged in the activity at all times and in a variety of roles. When students are not the interpreter, they might be primarily responsible for setting up and/or monitoring the video camera, observing a team member to provide feedback, providing backup support to the student who is working, timing the role-play, or keeping time so that each of the students scheduled to interpret during the role-play gets a turn. Arranging or confirming and preparing for these various responsibilities can also happen during the pre-role-play setup time.

The Role-Play Process

Once the participants are prepared to begin and the room is ready for the start of the role-play, the participants and students need to be introduced to one another. Introductions can be relatively brief, as long as those students who will be interpreting have the opportunity to preconference with participants by asking questions about the upcoming interaction. Including the preconferencing in the role-play process itself can be very useful in the post-role-play discussion because the number and types of questions students ask can make a difference in how prepared they are (either topic-wise or in terms of gaining familiarity with the participants' language use and conversational style). The introductions and preconferencing portion of the role-play will likely last 10–20 minutes.

When all parties are ready to begin, the teacher should mark the beginning of the role-play, and the camera should be turned on (if it has not already been). Even though the length of time of the actual role-play will vary depending on the number of students, the length of class meeting time, and so forth, all participants should have an idea of how much time has been allotted for the interaction. A good average for the length of the interaction would be 20–30 minutes. This seems to be enough time for the interaction to include an opening, a body, and a closing, which are common features of interactive discourse. The teacher or timekeeper can assist in

letting interpreters know when to switch (if applicable) and in letting participants know when it is time to conclude.

Post-Role-Play Discussions

After the interaction has concluded, there are at least two opportunities for useful discussion. The first is to ask those directly involved
what they thought about the interaction. Even though participants
might not use academic terminology, they are likely to comment on
relevant features. For example, participants might indicate that they
felt uncertain about when it was appropriate to take a turn or about
who was responsible for certain utterances (the interpreter or another participant). This feedback is very useful for students, who
should be able to discuss the issues in terms of the features studied
in class. This discussion can last 10–15 minutes. If time allows and
if there are any aspects of the interaction that were not wholly satisfactory, the role-play can be redone with appropriate adjustments.
For example, if the interpreting student simultaneously signed and
spoke an introduction of himself/herself at the beginning of the
role-play and found it difficult, this could be redone in another way
to see if it is more satisfactory, perhaps handling the introductions
in one language at a time (see Metzger 1995, 1999). When the role-
play and discussion with participants are complete, it is time for the
invited participants to leave, filling out any required invoice before
they go (if they will be paid).

The class-only discussion can then begin. This is a time when students can discuss what they observed about the interaction in more
specific detail with more technical terminology. The students who
actually interpreted the role-play should have the first opportunity
to express their views of the event. The discussion should address
what features of interaction occurred during the role-play, what
strategies the interpreting students employed, what seemed to work
well, and what could have been handled differently. This discussion
will probably take 10–20 minutes. If the role-play is done at a community site, the discussion might need to be postponed until after
the role-play site has been dismantled (cameras put away, chairs re-
turned, etc.). It can then be held in a space at the site if available or

back in the classroom either immediately or at the beginning of the next session. Students can also be required to turn in a written analysis of their observations. In fact, the students who have actually interpreted the role-play should definitely provide a written analysis of their work.

Student Analyses

Student analyses of their interactive interpretations will incorporate the analysis of the interpretation itself in terms of language production and equivalence. These will be relevant in both languages, of course. In addition, the analyses should focus on interactive issues. For example, if overlap occurred in the interaction, how did the interpreting student handle it? Was it always ignored? Were a variety of strategies used? Did the student tend to yield the turn always to the hearing participant? These are the details from which each student can develop individual goals to apply in the next role-play, and students should be expected to comment on how they are progressing over time (see Figure 3 for a sample student analysis form).

Conclusion

Even though a role-play can never completely simulate real life, careful planning can make role-plays a far more effective teaching strategy than either videotapes or practicing on real people in actual interpreting jobs. Interpreting students can be taught to be consciously aware of features unique to interactive discourse and the strategies interpreters use to cope with them. This awareness then serves as the foundation for making the live, interactive role-play an effective learning experience as students begin to apply what they have studied.

The use of carefully orchestrated role-plays is also very timely because researchers are increasingly finding that interpreters are not simply relayers of the monologic discourse of others. In daily conversation without interpreters, participants who share a language have been found to play a far more active role even as addressees

Live Source   Videotaped Source: cold   warm (_____x)

Source Text:

The source text was:

	1	2	3	4	5
a.	consecutive				simultaneous
b.	relatively slow				relatively fast
c.	easy to interpret				difficult to interpret

Explain your answer to c:

Interpretation Analysis:	English-to-ASL	ASL-to-English

Language Production:

Equivalence:

Interactive Issues—Interactional management:
Introductions

Summonses/attention-getting strategies

Turn taking and overlap

Responses to questions

Interactive Issues—Relayings:
Source attribution

Requests for clarification

Relaying of pronominal reference

than once thought (see Tannen 1989). Recognition of this joint negotiation of interactive discourse has led to studies that demonstrate that interpreters, too, play a more active role in interaction than was once thought to be the case. Because interpreters can no longer be seen as conduits to a dialogue between others (Roy 1989), interpreter education can not teach interpreters to simply relay the utterances of others. Interpreting students must learn how to participate in the conversation appropriately as an interpreter, perhaps as a third participant (Wadensjö 1992) or even as the second part of a dialogic interaction with each of the other participants, with the interpreter as the pivotal overlapping participant in each (Metzger 1995, 1999). Students of interpretation must learn not only how to interpret but specifically how to interpret interactive discourse.

Learning to interpret interaction requires that students learn about the relationship or alignment between themselves as interpreters and other participants. The ways in which interpreters relay pronouns, for example, can favor the use of first person for one participant and not for another (Metzger 1995, 1999). Interpreters can use certain types of strategies with one participant and not with another. For example, if students respond to the questions of one participant and not another, this can have an unintended impact on interactional outcomes (Metzger 1995, 1999). Doctors who feel out of control might not spend as much time with a patient, resulting in less than satisfactory services or diagnoses. Student interpreters can be taught early to recognize what strategies they have as options and to become aware of which strategies they choose. Appropriately designed role-plays provide an avenue for this aspect of an interpreter's education.

Interpreting students can also be taught that they will be generating their own utterances when interpreting in interactive settings. This does not necessarily mean that such self-generated utterances are as unconstrained as those of other participants. As a social role, interpreters are present in the interaction to accomplish a certain task and provide a professional service. The interpreter's utterances should be supportive of this. Moreover, not generating utterances has equal potential to be disruptive to an interaction. For example, not answering questions directed at the interpreter leaves an unfilled slot in a commonly occurring structure of interaction: the question–answer adjacency pair. By examining the structural features of interactive discourse, interpreters can learn how to respond to a variety of situations that arise in interpreted interactions. Appropriately designed role-plays provide an opportunity for interpreting students to develop these skills.

A role-play is not an easy teaching strategy because it is somewhat unpredictable. Nevertheless, carefully orchestrated role-plays can be designed to simulate aspects of real-world interaction. This can be accomplished, in part, by involving community members in role-plays that relate to their areas of expertise or in which they have a special interest. This can be accomplished as well by utilizing participants such as actors or drama students, who are skilled at generating features of interactive discourse upon demand. Providing interpreting students with information about interactive discourse and the coping strategies used by interpreters and designing role-plays in which they can apply this knowledge can prepare them not only for a future of videotaped assessments but also for the real world of interactive interpreting.

REFERENCES

Frishberg, N. 1990. *Interpreting: An introduction.* Silver Spring, Md.: RID Publications.

Goffman, E. 1981. *Forms of talk.* Philadelphia: University of Pennsylvania Press.

Labov, W. 1972. *Sociolinguistic patterns.* Philadelphia: University of Pennsylvania Press.

Mather, S. 1994. Adult/deaf toddler discourse. In *Post-Milan ASL and English literacy: Issues, trends, and research,* ed. B. Snider, 283–97. Washington, D.C.: Gallaudet University College for Continuing Education.

Metzger, M. 1995. The paradox of neutrality: A comparison of interpreters' goals with the realities of interactive discourse. Ph.D. diss., Georgetown University, Washington, D.C.

———. 1999. *Sign language interpreting: Deconstructing the myth of neutrality.* Washington, D.C.: Gallaudet University Press.

Roy, C. 1989. A sociolinguistic analysis of the interpreter's role in the turn exchanges of an interpreted event. Ph.D. diss., Georgetown University,

Washington, D.C.

———. 1993. A sociolinguistic analysis of the interpreter's role in simultaneous talk in interpreted interaction. *Multilingua* 12 (4): 341–63.

Sacks, H., E. Schegloff, and G. Jefferson. 1974. A simplest systematics for the organization of turn taking in conversation. *Language* 50:696–735.

Schegloff, E. 1972. Sequencing in conversational openings. In *Directions in sociolinguistics*, ed. J. Gumperz and D. Hymes, 346–80. New York: Holt, Rinehart, and Winston.

Schegloff, E., and H. Sacks. 1973. Opening up closings. *Semiotica* 7 (4): 289–327.

Seleskovitch, D. 1978. *Interpreting for international conferences: Problems of language and communication.* Washington, D.C.: Pen and Booth.

Tannen, D. 1984. *Conversational style: Analyzing talk among friends.* Norwood, N.J.: Ablex.

———. 1986. *That's not what I meant.* New York: Ballantine Books.

———. 1989. *Talking voices: Repetition, dialogue, and imagery in conversational discourse.* Cambridge: Cambridge University Press.

Wadensjö, C. 1992. *Interpreting as interaction: On dialogue interpreting in immigration hearings and medical encounters.* Linköping University: Linköping Studies in Arts and Sciences.

Zimmer, J. 1989. ASL/English interpreting in an interactive setting. In *Proceedings of the 30th Annual Conference of the American Translators Association*, ed. D. Hammond, 225–31. Medford, N.J.: Learned Information.

APPENDIX 1

Supplemental Readings on Interactive Discourse

Baker, C. 1977. Regulators and turn taking in American Sign Language discourse. In *On the other hand: New perspectives on American Sign Language*, ed. L. Friedman, 215–36. New York: Academic Press.

Hatch, E. 1992. *Discourse and language education*. Cambridge: Cambridge University Press.

Mather, S. 1996. Initiation in visually constructed dialogue: Reading books with three-to-eight-year-old students who are Deaf and hard of hearing. In *Multicultural aspects of sociolinguistics in Deaf communities*, ed. C. Lucas, 109–131. Washington, D.C.: Gallaudet University Press.

Metzger, M. 1995. The paradox of neutrality: A comparison of interpreters' goals with the realities of interactive discourse. Ph.D. diss., Georgetown University, Washington, D.C.

———. 1999. *Sign language interpreting: Deconstructing the myth of neutrality*. Washington, D.C.: Gallaudet University Press.

Roy, C. 1989. A sociolinguistic analysis of the interpreter's role in the turn exchanges of an interpreted event. Ph.D. diss., Georgetown University, Washington, D.C.

———. 1993. A sociolinguistic analysis of the interpreter's role in simultaneous talk in interpreted interaction. *Multilingua* 12 (4): 341–63.

Tannen, D. 1986. *That's not what I meant*. New York: Ballantine Books.

Wadensjö, C. 1992. *Interpreting as interaction: On dialogue-interpreting in immigration hearings and medical encounters*. Linköping University: Linköping Studies in Arts and Sciences.

Winston, E. 1993. Spatial mapping in comparative discourse frames in an American Sign Language lecture. Ph.D. diss., Georgetown University, Washington, D.C.

Zimmer, J. 1989. ASL/English interpreting in an interactive setting. In *Proceedings of the 30th Annual Conference of the American Translators Association*, ed. D. Hammond, 225–31. Medford, N.J.: Learned Information.

JEFFREY E. DAVIS

Translation Techniques in Interpreter Education

THE BASIS for using translation techniques in interpreter preparation is that translation provides an important framework for teaching and learning the interpreting process. This approach allows
interpretation to be taught as a series of successive learning situations that are critically linked to translation skills. In this systematic
approach to teaching interpreting, translation forms the basis for
consecutive interpretation, which precedes simultaneous interpretation. This teaching technique is particularly useful in helping students to get beyond the lexical and phrasal level (i.e., the surface
structures) to the deeper levels of semantics, pragmatics, and semiotics. Because simultaneous interpretation involves time constraints
and pressures, students are not always able to consciously focus on
specific components of the process. The goal becomes one of "keeping up," which sometimes means the loss of message accuracy and
linguistic purity.

Teaching translation and consecutive interpretation as the foundation for simultaneous interpretation allows students to expand the
skills involved in the interpreting process (e.g., concentration, visualization, short-term memory, and target language restructuring).
Most important, this strategy teaches that the interpreter must understand not only the intended meaning of the source text but also
the manner in which the audience is likely to understand the target
language.

Following Cokely (1992) the metaphor for interpreters in the
1990s has been one of *linguistic and cultural mediation*. Roy (1989,
2000) argues that interpreting is an interactive, face-to-face,

109

communicative event and that the interpreter's role is active, governed by social and linguistic knowledge of the entire communicative situation. This involves not only linguistic and cultural competence but also the appropriate ways of speaking and managing the intercultural event of interpreting. Interpreting between structurally different languages in which the users of the languages being interpreted hold different worldviews is one of the challenges of teaching and learning interpretation. Practitioners and educators agree that interpreters must make certain linguistic and cultural adjustments to accurately convey meaning. However, there has not been adequate examination of the strategies that interpreters use to accomplish this task. Furthermore, teaching strategies for this crosslinguistic and cross-cultural phenomenon have not been adequately described.

The primary focus of this chapter is on translation as a teaching technique in interpreter preparation. Again, the premise here is that teaching interpretation involves a series of successive learning situations that are critically linked to translation skills. Furthermore, this chapter describes specific techniques and strategies that can be used to teach students of interpreting, particularly, how to make appropriate linguistic and cultural adjustments. To begin with, it is necessary to clarify some of the meanings associated with translation/translating and interpretation/interpreting. Although most discussions of interlingual communication emphasize the distinction between translating and interpreting, both essentially involve the same basic underlying principles. The work of semioticians and developments in pragmatics have brought us closer to a unified theory of interlingual communication, in this case, a greater understanding of general translation and interpretation processes. This brings us to a greater understanding of the essential similarities and differences between translating and interpreting.

ISSUES OF DEFINITION

The terms *translation* and *interpretation* are frequently used interchangeably, for they share the common goal of transferring a mes-

sage between two languages. Despite the shared goal, however, practitioners use the two terms to denote distinctive activities: practices
and techniques. In fact, both translators and interpreters have their
own distinct professional organizations. Practitioners typically use
translation to describe linguistic conversion involving written texts,
whereas *interpretation* is used to denote the unrehearsed (that is, un-
written) conversion of a message from the source language into the
target language. The general convention, and the one that will be
used throughout this chapter, is that translation and interpretation
both refer to the general underlying process whereby meaning from
one language is transferred to another language regardless of the
form of either language (written, spoken, or signed).

Whereas interpreters are required to simultaneously or consecutively interpret the message from one language to another, translators, who are working primarily with written texts, often have the
luxury of time to accomplish their task. Interpretation describes the
process whereby the interpreter renders the source language message into the target language at approximately the same time as the
source message is being delivered (simultaneously) or in chunks
of discourse at varying time intervals following the delivery of
the source message (consecutively). The major difference, then, between translating and interpreting is the time allowed to accomplish
the transfer of meaning and the linguistic medium of the source
and/or target text (spoken/signed vs. written). The theoretical assumption here is that translation forms the basis for interpretation
and that consecutive interpretation is a prerequisite for simultaneous interpretation. Interpreter preparation, therefore, is a developmental process.

Toward a Common Theoretical Framework

A systematic approach to interpreter education, in which translation, intralingual communication skills, and consecutive interpreting are taught as prerequisite skills to simultaneous interpretation is
considered here to be one of the best practices in interpreter preparation. To explain how translation informs interpreting practice,

this chapter links the theory of translation to the practice of interpreting. A unified theory of interlingual communication is needed to account for the essential similarities and differences between translating and interpreting. Translation theory provides an important framework for teaching and learning the interpreting process.

The development of a theory of translation has benefited greatly from the work of semioticians, from developments in pragmatics, and from advances in the study of bilingualism and multilingualism. Scholars (most notably, Jakobson 1959, Ludskanov 1975, Bassnett–McGuire 1980, Oller 1989, and Givon 1989) have emphasized that the study of the translation process belongs most properly to *semiotics*, the science that studies sign systems or structures, sign processes, and sign functions.

The goal of translation, interpretation, and transliteration is first and foremost the transfer of meaning from a *source language* into a *target language*. This is accomplished by way of *semiotic transformation*, that is, changing the linguistic signs of the first language to the linguistic signs of the second language while accurately conveying the intended meaning. Simply put, the forms of each language, also referred to as the *surface structures*, are changed while meaning is transferred and held constant. Givon (1989, 324) defines the translation process as "the transfer of knowledge across major linguistic-cultural boundaries." Interpreter educators can testify that it is sometimes a challenge to get students to go beyond the lexical and phrasal levels (i.e., the surface structures) to the deeper levels of semantics, pragmatics, and semiotics. Interpreting pedagogy, therefore, must reflect principles of translation as they concern the interpreting process.

Four decades ago, Roman Jakobson (1959) distinguished three types of translation that still constitute important stages in the teaching of interpretation. These categories of translation are the following:

1. *Intralingual translation*, or rewording (an interpretation of verbal signs by means of other signs in the same language)
2. *Interlingual translation* or translation proper (an interpretation of verbal signs by means of some other language)

3. *Intersemiotic translation* (an interpretation of verbal signs by means of signs or nonverbal systems).

Jakobson maintains that *complete equivalence* in terms of synonymy or sameness cannot take place in any of three categories. The equivalency issue remains one of the central issues in translation and interpretation.

Beyond the notion that translation is the simple transfer of meaning contained in one set of linguistic signs into another set of linguistic signs is that the process also involves a whole set of extralinguistic criteria (e.g., the conveyance of the cultural context and nonverbal communication signals). Oller (1989), for one, points out that *pragmatics*, which is the study of how texts are linked up with corresponding facts in experience, also plays a major role in understanding the translation/interpretation process. Central to the theory of pragmatics is the notion of context and that reality and/or experience is frame-dependent, that is, dependent upon the observer's point of view (Givon 1989). Furthermore, translation is possible only to the extent that cross-cultural understanding is possible. Undoubtedly, translation, understanding, and culture are central to the interpreting process, and the pragmatic approach is well suited to interpreting pedagogy.

Along these lines, Givon (1989, 1–2) gives three metaphors for pragmatics as a method:

1. *Description and point of view:* The *description* of an entity is incomplete, indeed uninterpretable, unless it specifies the *point of view* from whence the description was undertaken;
2. *Picture and frame:* A picture is not fully specified unless its *frame* is also specified;
3. *Meaning and context:* The *meaning* of an expression cannot be fully understood without understanding the *context* in which the expression is used (original emphasis).

Pragmatics teaches that in order for meaning to be properly framed, the interpreter has the dual task of fully comprehending the source message meaning *and* the context for which the message is intended. This is accomplished through semiotic transformation.

Semiotic transformation means that one must be able to distinguish both between the objects signified by the words from the source and target languages and between the functional value of those objects in the source and target culture. This involves the dual task of understanding the meaning of the source text and the manner in which the audience is likely to comprehend it in the target language. The interpreter, therefore, is not a passive "conduit" of information. Students must learn that the interpreting process involves a great deal of decision making at all levels of discourse.

THE EQUIVALENCY ISSUE

Two issues that frequently arise in translation/interpretation studies are *equivalency* and *cultural untranslatability*. Again, the study of pragmatics and semiotics sheds light on these issues. Highly skilled translators, interpreters, and other individuals who are bilingual or multilingual make the transfer between languages through semiotic transformation. In other words, these individuals successfully make the linguistic and cultural adjustments necessary to convey meaning accurately. That is, they are able to successfully translate. From the semiotic perspective, words and other expressions are held to be signs that signify things by way of mediating concepts. The challenge is to teach students how to cross the pragmatic gulf between different languages and cultures. Translation practice is an excellent way to teach the importance of context and culture (pragmatics) and how to go beyond the lexical level to deeper levels of cultural and linguistic meaning (semiotics).

In translation studies, it has long been recognized that there is not a one-to-one correspondence or equivalency between the linguistic forms of two different languages (Jakobson 1959, Mounin 1963, Nida and Taber 1969, Bassnett–McGuire 1980, Larson 1984). This is what Saussure meant when he referred to "the arbitrariness of the linguistic sign" that is, the conventionality of the relationship between form and meaning. Givon (1989, 328) has gone so far as to say that "given the manifest cultural-linguistic diversity, 'real' translation is not possible." That is, even though it is possible for the interpreter/translator to discover the meaning of the source language and reexpress the meaning into the target language, there is ordinarily no full equivalence. Practitioners and educators know that even apparent synonymy does not yield equivalence and often that a combination of lexical items must be used in order to accurately interpret the meaning of a single word. Interpreter educators frequently find students who are confused and dismayed by this basic linguistic fact. As educators, we sometimes find ourselves hard pressed to come up with a simple translation for a single vocabulary item presented to us by a student. How many times have we said to our students, "There simply is no one-to-one correspondence for that word" or "It depends on the context."

Nonetheless, the notions of real translation and full equivalency should not be misconstrued. Much evidence supports that translation in practice is generally successful, even when carried out between languages that are typologically different. Thus, it simply would not be true to say that translation is not possible. Nida and Taber (1969, 1982) and Seleskovitch (1978) emphasize that translation *is* obtainable, regardless of the languages involved, insofar as the translator or interpreter is *able to understand and adjust for form, meaning, and context between the languages and cultures with which they work*. Again, here we see the meaning of "linguistic and cultural mediation."

THE IMMEDIATE AND DELIBERATE DISCARDING OF WORDS

Some words have direct equivalents from one language to another just as some words are untranslatable, that is, they do not have a word-for-word equivalence (though the latter is more often the case than the former). Herein lies the challenge: The interpreter/translator must transcend the purely linguistic surface forms, analyze the source language text for meaning, and restructure the message into the target language. Seleskovitch (1978, 84–85), for example, points out that "two concepts are often confused when people speak of 'untranslatable' words: the concept of *translating* in the sense of transposing from one language to another by substituting one word for another, and that of *expressing* the same thing in two languages (original emphasis)." In sum, almost all words would be untranslatable if translation were taken to mean a word-for-word equivalence without regard for context.

As Seleskovitch (1978) puts it:

> Suppose one could move from one language to another by using a simple word-for-word translation without relying on the intelligence of the person "translating": this would be tantamount to admitting that languages have an objective existence of their own, that they function independently and that the form of the message and the information conveyed are identical. (86)

Because interpretation is a process whereby the source language message is immediately changed into the target language, the task requires comprehension of the source language input, *immediate discarding of words* from the source language, analysis of the source message for meaning, and restructuring the source message into the target language output. Again, the interpreter must understand not only the meaning of the source text *but also the manner in which the audience for which the text is intended is likely to understand it in the target language.*

This endeavor is even more challenging when the two languages involved are different structurally, such as English–Russian, Navajo–Japanese, Finnish–Spanish, or English–American Sign Language (ASL). English–ASL interpretation, for example, involves not only two structurally different languages but also two different linguistic modalities (aural/oral in contrast to visual/gestural). If the situation were not complex enough, it is further complicated when one language enjoys greater status and wider use than the other and where the native speakers of each language hold different cultural views. There are also majority/dominant language and minority language issues that must be considered. The general principles outlined in this chapter can be applied regardless of the languages or cultures involved.

FROM ONE TO MANY AND FROM MANY TO ONE

There are many examples that educators can use to teach students the complexities of transferring meaning between languages. Even the most simple, straightforward examples warrant careful consideration. Consider, for example, interpreting *yes* and *hello* into French, German, and Italian (data from Bassnett–McGuire, 1980, 16–17). For translation of the English word *yes*, standard dictionaries give the following:

French: oui; si

German: ja

Italian: si

First, the existence of the two terms in French represent usage not found in the other languages. That is, whereas *oui* is generally used to convey affirmation, *si* is used to convey contradiction, contention, and dissent. Further, *yes* cannot always be translated with the single words *oui*, *ja*, or *si*. French, German, and Italian frequently reduplicate affirmatives in a different way from English, for example, oui, oui, oui; ja, ja, ja; si, si, si. Bassnett–McGuire (1980, 17) points out that "the Italian or German translation of *yes* by a single word can, at times, appear excessively brusque, whilst the stringing together of affirmatives in English is so hyperbolic that it often creates a comic effect."

For the translation of the English greeting *hello*, dictionaries give the following:

French: ç a va?; hallo

German: wie geht's? hallo

Italian: ola; pronto; ciao

In contrast to English, which makes no distinction between the word used for greeting someone in person and that used when answering the telephone, French, German, and Italian all do make that distinction. According to Bassnett–McGuire (1980), *pronto* in

Italian and *hallo* in German function strictly as telephone greetings; French and German use rhetorical questions as greetings that would be considered formal in English, such as, "How do you do?"; and *ciao* is used in Italian as a greeting as well as in departure. Thus, language forms as basic as affirmations and greetings have different functions and meanings according to the cultural context in which they are being used. This basic fact demonstrates the need for linguistic and cultural adjustments.

As another example, consider the different language forms used to convey the meaning "a person, who is the speaker, possesses money": English uses "I have money"; Japanese and Latin use forms that literally say "to me there is money"; Arabic and Russian use forms that say "with me there is money"; and Turkish uses forms that say "my money exists" (examples from Larson, 1984, 5). These complex configurations of form and meaning present a challenge to individuals translating or interpreting between languages. The examples provided here are not intended to exhaust the possible range of meanings conveyed by words or phrases between languages but are presented to illustrate one of the universal characteristics of language referred to here as "from one to many and from many to one" (Davis and Jankowski 1994). That is, a single word in one language may have several different meanings; a single meaning may be conveyed by multiple lexical items; or a word in one language will need to be translated by several words or vice versa. This is not limited to lexical items but is also true for phrases that may express several different meanings. These examples and others like them can demonstrate to students of interpretation that in transferring meaning, the interpreter/translator must make the appropriate word choices and consider all levels of meaning—lexical, syntactic, semantic, and pragmatic—in the process.

Clearly, interpreting/translating is much more than the simple encoding of linguistic forms from the source language to the target language. Successful interpretation requires understanding the multilingual/multicultural dimensions of the interpreting context. Furthermore, interpreting between structurally different languages in which the native users of the languages being interpreted hold different worldviews creates additional challenges. The intensive and prolonged contact between ASL and English has resulted in a very complex set of multilingual and multicultural issues. Signed language interpreters may also be expected to transliterate (that is, code ASL signs into English word order). They may also encounter manual codes for English (artificially developed sign language systems designed to represent English visually) and may be expected to sign and speak simultaneously (the equivalent of trying to speak two different languages simultaneously).

English contains numerous words that have multiple meanings, depending on their context (*run* and *have* are just two examples). According to some accounts (e.g., the *Reader's Digest Great Encyclopedic Dictionary*), fifty-four meanings exist for the English word *run*. As discussed earlier, other languages may use different words to convey each of the different meanings. Table 1 shows the ASL equivalents for some English words, and the table's examples demonstrate that words consist of bundles of meanings. As Larson (1984, 6) puts it, "Meaning components are 'packaged' into lexical items, but they are 'packaged' differently in one language than in another."

These are but a few examples of how a combination of lexical forms must be used in order to provide a proximate equivalent. In summary, the most basic principle—that translation involves a great deal more than the simple replacement of lexical and grammatical items between languages—is grounded in semiotic theory. Therefore, in order for meaning to be conveyed, the interpreter/translator must transcend the purely linguistic surface forms by way of *linguistic and cultural mediation*. Neubert (1967), for one, in an attempt to solve the problem of equivalence, postulates that translation equivalence is a *semiotic category* comprising syntactic, semantic, and pragmatic components. Neubert places these components in a hierarchical relationship in which semantic equivalence takes priority over syntactic equivalence and in which pragmatic equivalence conditions and modifies both semantic and syntactic elements. Equivalence, therefore, is obtainable from the relationship between signs and what they stand for and also from the interaction between signs and what they stand for to those who use them.

Table 1. ASL Equivalents for English Words with Multiple Meanings

English Term	ASL Equivalent
Call	
My friends call me Bob.	NAME
Call me when you get home.	CALL-ON-PHONE or CALL-ON-TDD (depending on context)
Call for help.	TO-CALL-OUT-FOR (similar form for SHOUT or SCREAM)
Call in the next patient.	TO-SUMMON
Have	
I have a new car. (possessive)	TO-POSSESS
I have been to Europe. (auxiliary)	FINISH
I have not been to Europe. (auxiliary)	LATE
I have to go now. (modal)	MUST
Run	
They had a run in with each other.	CONFLICT OR CONFRONT-EACH-OTHER
Are you going to run in the marathon?	TO RUN (there are different regional forms for this use of run)
She had a run in her stocking.	CLASSIFIER "run in stocking"
Do you think she will run for president?	TO-APPLY

To date, however, there has not been adequate examination or description of the strategies that interpreters use to successfully accomplish this task, nor has there been adequate discussion of the fact that it requires pragmatic knowledge of the multilingual/multicultural contexts in which interpreting takes place. The multidimensional aspects of the interpreting context must be reflected in the interpreting training curriculum. Specific exercises that teach students of interpretation how to bridge linguistic and cultural gaps that occur in the process of transferring meaning between languages are presented in the next section.

Translation Techniques in Interpreter Education

Some curriculum decisions need to be made when considering how to incorporate translation studies into an interpreting preparation program. Some programs offer a specific translation course or courses, whereas others incorporate translation activities in the advanced stages of language preparation and continue to "spiral" these activities throughout the interpreting curriculum. Translation may be used as a form of evaluation, and translation activities may be included throughout various stages of the interpreter-preparation process. The translation techniques described here are more effective following certain prerequisites: first, completion or advanced placement in the language preparation portion of the curriculum; second, completion of a formal course in translation or extensive translation practice during the language preparation stages of the program; third, development of intralingual skills (such as shadowing, paraphrasing, and abstracting); fourth, practice in giving and receiving feedback; and fifth, a basic understanding of translation theory (for example, issues of equivalency and cultural untranslatability) and of the basic interpreting process.

Choosing Texts

The initial preparation for this activity is to gather source language texts. For this purpose the instructor should select source language texts that exhibit the following features:

1. A variety of contexts and registers
2. Naturally occurring discourse (frozen texts may also be used)
3. Various linguistic models (e.g., young and old, male and female, and culturally, ethnically, and linguistically diverse)
4. A wide range of linguistic expressions that are metaphorical, idiomatic, and figurative and have worldviews embedded within "ways of speaking."

Texts should range from monologic (one speaker) to dialogic (interactive). The original source language texts should be audio- or videotaped. Ideally, the instructor should have written transcriptions of the source language texts. Commercially produced materials or materials produced by the Regional Interpreter Training Consortium (RITC) are readily available and may be adapted for this activity. For illustration purposes, here is an excerpt from the "Interactive Interpreting Series" produced through the RITC grant at Gallaudet University, Department of ASL, Linguistics, and Interpretation. The following example is from a videotaped interview between a real estate agent (REA) and an ASL signing Deaf consumer (DC):

> REA: Chuck, so nice to meet you. Robert has told me so much about you.
> DC: *Nice to meet you, too. Robert told me you were really a big help to him.*
> REA: I hope we were, and I'm hoping we can do the same for you. Robert says you are moving here from another part of the country.
> DC: *That's right—from L.A.*
> REA: Have you had an opportunity yet to check the Washington area out much for houses?
> DC: *Yes, I have been driving around the area taking a look at the houses in the metro area for a couple of weeks now, and I think I like Maryland best because of the easy commute to work.*

In this text, students discover that even simple greetings require careful consideration when being translated and also become aware of several regional signs for specific geographic locations.

Students must have an opportunity to discuss different ways of dealing with the figurative use of language during translation or interpretation. In the process, students learn that there are several options to deal with figurative and idiomatic language. First, the figurative expression may be literally translated word for word; second, depending on the audience and setting, the figurative expression may be translated word for word followed by an explanation of its meaning; third, the meaning may be simply translated without

Table 2. Sample Translations of Figurative Language

Type of Translation	English	ASL Translation
Word for Word	Hold your horses	Literal translation
Word for word with explanation	A bird in the hand is worth two in the bush	Explanation of meaning
Translation without equivalent imagery	Make a mountain out of a mole hill	EXAGGERATE
Equivalent or near-equivalent	Sorry, you missed the boat	TRAIN-ZOOM GONE SORRY
	Raining cats and dogs	BUCKET POURING-DOWN

keeping the original idiomatic form or metaphoric imagery; or fourth, the original figurative expression may be translated by using an equivalent or near-equivalent figurative expression or metaphor from the target language (cf. Larson 1984). Table 2 contains samples of these types of translations.

PREPARING MODEL TRANSLATIONS

Once source language texts are selected, model translations into the target language are prepared. Native users of the target language and/or professional interpreters are used as models. These individuals are then presented with the written transcription of the source language text from which to prepare a target language translation. The models are videotaped or audiotaped translating source language texts into the target language. It is useful to prepare at least two target language models for each source language text. The teacher and students then use these target language models for comparative and text analysis purposes. In addition, commercially produced materials or materials produced through the Regional Interpreter Training Consortium may be used.

TRANSLATION IN ACTION

To begin the translation activity, the class is divided into groups of three. In each group, one student role-plays the interpreter, a second the consumer, and the third monitors the interpreting process. The members of each triad may be assigned a letter (A, B, C or X, Y, Z) or a number (1, 2, 3) to facilitate the turn-taking process. Students take turns role-playing the interpreter, consumer, or monitor of the process. This approach maximizes interpreting practice for each class participant. In preparation for this activity, students learn to articulate the translation/interpretation process, the importance of teamwork, and how to give and receive meaningful feedback. They also learn to identify linguistic miscues, such as additions, deletions, intrusions, and substitutions, in the target language production of the source language text (cf. Cokely 1992).

For example, the translation activity may be sequenced in the following way:

1. Each group (triad) is given the written transcription and context of the source language text. Depending on the length of the text, the group is given 3–5 minutes to talk together to create a translation of the text. Particular attention is given to linguistic and cultural adjustments they need to make.

2. One student from each group then assumes the interpreter role. The second student in the group role-plays the consumer, and the third student takes notes for discussion and feedback.

3. The instructor plays an audio- or videotape of the source language text, and then students individually listen to the entire chunk of discourse.

4. Students in the interpreter role (i.e., 1, 2, or 3) then give the translation of the source language text into the target language.

5. All students observe, discuss what was easy or challenging, and talk about their choices and what they would change. The students give and receive feedback about the target language translation and translation process.

6. The instructor then shows one or two model translations/interpretations of the same source text into the target language.

Students compare and discuss similarities and differences between the different translations.

There are also several variations of this teaching technique. For example, the written transcripts can be used to practice sight translation, or students can practice translating the target language models back into the source language (i.e., back translation). Texts can be presented in written or audio- or videotaped formats.

SAMPLE TEXTS

The following examples illustrate that the translation/interpretation process encompasses all levels of language. The first examples are from the "Semantic Awareness Assessment" produced by Sign Media, Inc. Each group of English sentences has one word in common (shown here in boldface). For this activity, students mentally translate each English sentence into ASL, view a target ASL sign on videotape, and decide in which translated sentence the target ASL sign would most likely be used. Here are a few examples:

1. a. This sales pitch **works** every time.
   b. I want a sandwich with the **works**.
   c. Mary **works** for a law firm downtown.
2. a. This is the **last** copy of the newspaper.
   b. I hope this situation doesn't **last** too long.
   c. I wasn't here at our **last** meeting.
3. a. He was nervous performing **before** a large audience.
   b. I've met him **before** at one of your parties.
   c. They assigned seats just **before** the break.

Each of the highlighted English lexical items requires a different ASL translation. This type of activity is an excellent way to assess semantic competency, develop beginning translation skills, and teach visualization skills.

Here are examples of simple English texts that students first translate into ASL and then view model ASL translations of the target sentences:

1. "I enjoy going out to eat every Friday. It sure beats having to cook."
2. "I ordered a blouse from Land's End, and I've been waiting for weeks and weeks for it to arrive. It finally arrived yesterday, and guess what? It was the wrong size."
3. "I didn't know that my aunt and uncle hated each other so much. That's why they were always fighting!"

The translation of each of these simple English texts requires complete syntactic restructuring. Students also discover that it is often necessary to receive the complete sentence or text before it can be accurately translated. In other words, simply lagging two or three words behind does not provide adequate context. They learn to back off from the text instead of following too closely. This exercise allows for greater processing time to convey meaning.

Moreover, in the first example, the metaphor "it sure beats having to cook" does not translate as a metaphor into ASL. Students must explore other options (such as the rhetorical clause) to successfully transfer meaning. In the second text, students observe gender differences in the ways a male or female native ASL user would express "waiting for weeks and weeks for a blouse and then discovering it was the wrong size." In the third text, for example, students observe that the ASL model translations incorporate a gesture that is considered obscene in mainstream society (specifically, the use of the middle finger). In the ASL translation, however, this gesture is inflected as a verb phrase for reciprocal agreement (i.e., "they hated each other so much"). Thus it does not carry the same connotations in the target culture as the general use of that gesture in the source culture.

Source language texts for these classroom activities may be acquired from a variety of sources: produced by the instructor, purchased commercially, or obtained through the Regional Interpreting Training Consortium (RITC). The following excerpt is from the previously mentioned videotaped interview between the real estate agent (REA) and the Deaf consumer (DC):

REA: What type of hobbies do you have? Do you have any special needs, say, for extra space? Maybe you're a photographer and need some developing . . . a developing room, or something like that?

DC: *I do have a hobby, I work with clay pottery. I have some equipment I use for that—you know—the wheel to make the pottery, and I also have a long table that I use for the finishing touches, the painting.*

REA: Okay, now is that something you could do in a basement?

DC: *Well, I don't want it to be in a dark area.*

REA: Well, now I have seen some properties where they have walk-out basements. Now there you have sliding glass doors, a couple of windows . . . would that be suitable?

DC: *Oh sure. If there's a lot of windows or a sliding glass door, that would be fine.*

This particular interactive text illustrates that the interpreter must have a clear visual representation of the source text in mind to accurately convey the message. In addition to teaching students about turn-taking issues (cf. Roy and Metzger, this volume), interpreting interactive discourse also teaches that there are certain discourse markers in the source language that do not necessarily get translated as a word-for-word equivalent in the target language. For example, in the preceding English text, words like *say, well, something like that, now,* or *okay* are not translated into ASL as single lexical items. Likewise, interpreters will also recognize that single ASL lexical items typically glossed as GULP, AWFUL , UNDERSTAND, and so on do not get translated literally into English. Each language requires different intonational and lexical devices to convey these crosslinguistic features of discourse. I hope that the preceding examples have demonstrated how the translation/interpretation process encompasses all levels of language—lexical, phrasal, and discourse.

TEACHING AND LEARNING OUTCOMES

The teaching technique that is the focus of this chapter leads to several learner outcomes. First, it demonstrates the critical link between theory and practice. Students of interpretation learn that translation theory provides guidelines and principles that apply directly to issues in interpreting practice. Specifically, it teaches interpreters to "break from form," which necessitates the immediate discarding of words. As students move beyond lexical and phrasal levels, they discover the principle that individual words are open to multiple meanings depending on content, context, speaker affect, style, register, and so on. This allows the classroom to become a laboratory for students to experiment with exactly what is meant by linguistic and cultural mediation. In essence, making appropriate linguistic and cultural adjustments is synonymous with successful translation or interpretation.

Translation practice also illuminates the interpreting process. Seleskovitch (1978, 9), for example, describes the interpreting process in three stages: first, apprehension of the language and message comprehension; second, "immediate discarding of the wording and retention of the mental representation of the message (concepts, ideas, etc.)"; and third, production of a new utterance in the target language that must both express the source message in its entirety and be geared to the audience. Through translation practice, students more fully experience what is meant by each stage of the interpreting process. They learn to focus on the target language message, more deeply experience or visualize what is meant by the message, and practice making linguistic and cultural adjustments to accurately convey the original meaning to the target language audience.

Most important, this activity provides models from which students can observe and create successful translations. This validates the work students have been doing and encourages them toward the goal of simultaneous interpretation. By observing different models, students see that there are various interpretations of the same utterance and that even the most proficient language users make linguistic miscues. This process allows participants to explore the options available to them. It encourages interpreting teamwork, clearer articulation of the interpreting process, and analysis of translation miscues in an objective manner. Participants learn to give and receive meaningful corrective and supportive feedback. They are usually able to identify exactly which part of the process may or may not be working during a particular translation. This systematic approach to teaching interpreting allows students to consciously focus on specific components of the process and experience successful interpretation firsthand.

SUMMARY

Translation theory teaches that a successful transfer of meaning between languages demands that the interpreter/translator make certain linguistic and cultural adjustments. This requires understanding the multilingual/multicultural dimensions of the interpreting context. Interpreting between structurally different languages in which the native users of the interpreted languages hold different worldviews is one of the great challenges of teaching, learning, and practicing interpretation. Translation practice is an excellent way to demonstrate that meanings not only reside in words but are also embedded in cultural and social contexts. Clearly, there are two central issues shared in translation and interpretation studies: equivalency (i.e., whether there is a one-to-one correspondence between the surface forms of different languages) and cultural untranslatability (i.e., understanding a language entails understanding the culture's worldview, and cross-language translation is possible only to the extent that cross-cultural translation is possible). The interpreter-training curriculum, therefore, must go beyond teaching lexicon and grammar to the levels of semantics, pragmatics, and semiotics. Only then can students of interpretation learn to function effectively across a range of multilingual/multicultural interpreting contexts.

REFERENCES

Bassnett–McGuire, S. 1980. *Translation studies*. London: Methuen.
Chernov, G. V. 1994. Message redundancy and message anticipation in simultaneous interpreting. In *Bridging the gap*, ed. S. Lambert and B. Moser–Mercer, 139–54. Amsterdam/Philadelphia: John Benjamins.
Cokely, D. 1992. *Interpretation: A sociolinguistic model*. Burtonsville, Md.: Sign Media.

Davis, J., and K. Jankowski. 1994. From one to many and from many to one: A comparative analysis of ASL and the English lexicon. In *The deaf way: Perspectives from the International Conference on Deaf Culture*, ed. C. J. Erting, R. C. Johnson, D. Smith, and B. Snider, 454–60. Washington, D.C.: Gallaudet University Press.

Givon, T. 1989. *Mind, code, and context: Essays in pragmatics*. Hillsdale, N.J.: Lawrence Erlbaum.

Jakobson, R. 1959. On linguistic aspects of translation. In *On translation*, ed. R. A. Brower. Cambridge, Mass.: Harvard University Press.

Kalina, S. 1994. Some views on the theory of interpreting training and some practical suggestions. In *Translation studies: An interdiscipline*, ed. M. Snell–Hornby, F. Pochhacker, and K. Kaindl, 219–25. Selected papers from the Translation Studies Congress, Vienna, September 9–12, 1992. Amsterdam/Philadelphia: John Benjamins. [Benjamins Translation Library, 2.]

Lambert, S. M. 1988. A human information processing and cognitive approach to the training of simultaneous interpreters. In *Languages at crossroads*, ed. D. L. Hammond, 379–87. Proceedings of the 29th Annual Conference of the American Translators Association (ATA), Seattle, Wash., October 12–16, 1988. Medford, N.J.: Learned Information.

Larson, M. L. 1984. *Meaning-based translation: A guide to cross-language equivalence*. New York: University Press of America.

Ludskanov, A. 1975. A semiotic approach to the theory of translation. *Language Sciences* 35 : 5–8.

Mikkelson, H. 1995. On the horns of a dilemma: Accuracy vs. brevity in the use of legal terms by court interpreters. In *Translation and the law*, ed. M. Morris, 208–18. Amsterdam/Philadelphia: John Benjamins. [American Translators Association (ATA) Monograph Series, VIII.]

———. 1996. Community interpreting: An emerging profession. *Interpreting* 1 : 125–29.

Mounin, G. 1963. *Les problèmes théoriques de la traduction*. Paris: Gallimard.

Neubert, A. 1967. *Elemente einer allgemeinen theorie der translation*. Actes du X Congrès International des Linguistes, Bucharest II. 451–56.

Nida, E., and C. Taber. 1969. *The theory and practice of translation*. Leiden: E. J. Brill. Reprinted 1982.

Oller, J. W., Jr. 1989. *Language and experience: Classic pragmatism*. Lanham, Md.: University Press of America.

Roy, C. B. 1989. A sociolinguistic analysis of the interpreter's role in the turn exchanges of an interpreted event. Ph.D. diss., Georgetown University, Washington, D.C.

———. 2000. *Interpreting as a discourse process*. New York: Oxford University Press.

Schweda Nicholson, N. 1993. An introduction to basic note-taking skills for consecutive interpretation. In *Interpreting: Yesterday, today, and tomorrow*, ed. D. Bowen and M. Bowen, 136–45. Binghamton, N.Y.: State University of New York. [American Translators Association (ATA) Scholarly Monograph Series, IV.]

Seleskovitch, D. 1978. *Interpreting for international conferences: Problems of language and communication*. Washington, D.C.: Pen and Booth.

Seleskovitch, D., and M. Lederer. 1995. *A systematic approach to teaching interpretation*, trans. J. Harmer. Silver Spring, Md.: Registry of Interpreters for the Deaf.

Weber, W. K. 1990. The importance of sight translation in an interpreter training program. In *Interpreting: Yesterday, today, and tomorrow*, ed. D. Bowen and M. Bowen, 44–52. Binghamton, N.Y.: State University of New York.

RICO PETERSON

Metacognition and Recall Protocols in the Interpreting Classroom

PERCEPTIONS OF literacy have undergone a remarkable change in the last half of the twentieth century. Where before, literacy was thought of as the ability to read and write, literacy today is construed as dynamic, as the ability to function in a language and culture. Agar (1994), finding it impossible to separate language from culture, coined the term *languaculture* to encompass the complexity of the issue. Building on the concept of literacy as the ability to function in a languaculture, biliteracy, then, the ability to function in two separate languacultures, can be seen as the sine qua non of a competent interpreter.

As disparate fields of knowledge in philosophy, psychology, sociology, anthropology, and linguistics have branched out and recombined into the domain of discourse, our notions of language have evolved as well. Discourse has been defined in a number of different ways. Some call it language "above the sentence level" (Hymes, as described in Schiffrin 1994, 23). Others describe it as "stretches of language perceived to be meaningful, unified, and purposive" (Cook 1989, 156). Still others see it as "the interpretation of the communicative event in context" (Nunan 1993, 6–7). Whatever perspective is taken, the study of discourse is an essential component in an interpreter training program.

The study of language, foreign or native, has been in retreat for years in the United States. Study after study shows that students

132

place little emphasis on learning a foreign language (Bartley 1970; Reinert 1970; Cohen 1977; Christison and Krahnke 1986; Ramage 1990; Roberts 1992; Oxford and Shearin 1994; Mantle–Bromley 1995). The current push for monolingual education is another indication of the low priority foreign language study is given. The study of English does not fare much better. Recent research shows that eighth-graders in the United States read more, do more homework, and ask more questions in the classroom than do their twelfth-grade counterparts (National Center for Education Statistics 1994). Language, it seems, is largely taken for granted by administrators and students alike.

Van Lier (1995) discusses the way the study of language has changed over the past several hundred years. From the time of the ancient Greeks until the late Middle Ages, the trivium of grammar, logic, and rhetoric formed the foundation upon which education was built. Since that time language has been slowly separated out from the core of study until it has become just another of the many subjects in the curriculum. Van Lier cites this as a possible reason for the apathy students frequently show in language study.

Yet language is likely as complex a system as humankind will ever devise. Learning a second language, then, especially in a classroom, is a prodigious task. The classroom is a notoriously inefficient place to learn language. An artificial environment, it is time-bound and often lacking in authentic language samples. Even when the teacher is a native speaker of the target language, the respective roles of teacher and student and the scripts of classroom behaviors and expectations often inhibit access to authentic, "natural" language samples.

Language learning is generally not a concern in spoken language interpreting programs, in which bilingual fluency is a minimum requirement for entrance. However, as the field of sign language interpreting grows, so does the number of students for whom the classroom is the initial, if not primary, source of language acquisition. Here it is not unusual for students to enter interpreting programs with as few as three or four semesters of language instruction behind them, sometimes even fewer. Sad to say, some programs even offer interpreting classes to students who are still in the early stages of learning to sign (see Jacobs [1996] for a thorough, and alarming, discussion on just how unprepared many sign language interpreting students are to undertake the study of interpreting). In spite of this, it is not unusual for students to try to accelerate their program, to "get the certificate" as quickly as possible.

In learning a language, as in interpreting, comprehension necessarily precedes production. Though few today would argue the post hoc nature of this relationship, the way we describe the process of acquisition is often at odds with our understanding of how it occurs. References abound to "learning to speak a language," whereas one rarely hears a comment such as "she can understand three languages." The teaching texts we employ often reinforce the view that language learning first and foremost means learning to speak it. Scores of books are devoted to teaching students "how to sign." In them one finds page after page filled with drawings intended to show how to produce signs. Some even include expository accounts of what each hand is doing at each moment. Little mention is made of comprehension, of how to understand the language.

Listening skills, reading comprehension, critical thinking skills— all staples of second language instruction in other languages—are largely absent from sign language curricula. This presents a crucial issue in teaching literacy skills to ASL students. Is this an indication that we do not know how to teach comprehension, or that we assume it occurs as a natural byproduct of observation or of being taught to sign? Reddy (1979) argues that the way we talk about language (or in this case, fail to talk about it) limits our ability to use language. Comprehension-based approaches to second language learning have shown remarkable potential, but these techniques are largely untried in sign language instruction.

Many sign language interpreter training programs find that students need a good deal of remedial English in addition to the remedial signing they require. This remediation ranges from the fundamentals of parts of speech to the intricacies of syntax. Text analysis is often employed as a means of educating students about how language works. Turning tacit awareness of language into explicit knowledge of form and function can pay real dividends in the interpreting classroom.

PROCESSING MEANING

A firm grounding in the fundamental aspects of language and discourse is instrumental to the development of metacognitive ability. *Metacognition* can be described simply as the knowledge we have about how our cognitive processes function. Where cognition is the process of knowing, metacognition is the awareness of *how* we know. Metacognition is crucial to the process of making meaning. Take, for example, this brief passage:

> Since he had written several scholarly books on the subject, we thought the professor's lecture would be sophisticated and serious, but all he offered was persiflage. Instead of the carefully crafted analysis of the subject we expected, we got nothing but trivial joking and banter.

The word *persiflage* may well be unfamiliar to the reader. However, most readers will have little difficulty in coming up with an adequate understanding of the word. One possible strategy for defining the unknown term goes like this: The word "but" tells us that persiflage is not something that is "sophisticated and serious." Because the "carefully crafted analysis of the subject" from the second sentence both refers to and is synonymous with the "lecture" in the first sentence, we might suspect that the "trivial joking and banter" is also a possible substitution for "persiflage." In this way we predict a working definition for the unknown word. As the discussion continues, we may check this definition against the new information we receive and adjust our definition accordingly. The process of hypothesizing and checking is one type of metacognitive strategy for processing information. This type of deductive reasoning, which works downward from the level of discourse to the level of the lexical item, is sometimes called *top-down processing*.

A different model for processing discourse works in exactly the opposite manner. *Bottom-up processing* starts with the lexical items and combines them into the next highest unit. These units, in turn, are combined into the next highest unit. For example, words become phrases, phrases become sentences, and sentences form texts. Clearly this is a much slower method of processing information. It is, however, very familiar to anyone who has tried to understand signing by attaching a word to every sign seen. This strategy is very common among beginning signers. The problem comes when an unfamiliar sign occurs, a sign for which there is no word available. This brings the processing to a screeching halt. With no new input and only the vague context of a string of unrelated words, comprehension breaks down and meaning is lost.

Another paradigm for processing that holds promise for the study of interpretation is called the interactive model. Interactive models were developed in response to perceived shortcomings in the top-down and bottom-up models. The interactive model suggests that listeners process discourse by using information from several levels simultaneously. In other words, comprehension is not simply unidirectional, top-down or bottom-up. This paradigm conceives of comprehension as a complex system of overlapping strategies. See Stanovich (1980) for a thorough review of language-processing models.

Metacognitive strategies for comprehending meaning have clear implications in the interpreting classroom. Because many students are still in the process of learning the language, tools for "repairing" incomplete information or for compensating for messages that are not clearly comprehended are especially useful.

ASSESSING COMPREHENSION

One of the difficulties in teaching ASL comprehension is assessment. Sign production is visible, and visible standards exist to which it can be held. It can be recorded and replayed, and this reproduction can be analyzed on a minute, frame-by-frame level. Comprehension, on the other hand, cannot be seen. Where signing can be evaluated in its natural medium, evaluating comprehension at all without removing it from its natural medium is difficult. Moreover, the instruments used to evaluate comprehension often add a layer of production that complicates the assessment.

Typical instruments, such as cloze, fill-in-the-blank, and short-answer questions, operate closer to the lexical, phrasal, or sentence level than to the discourse level. Thus they offer little real information about student ability to process discourse. Bernhardt (1991) makes a convincing argument against assessment techniques that employ a competing layer of text. The "text" of the questions asked confounds the measurement of raw comprehension. Moreover, in any given classroom, students are frequently at very different levels of competence, making it difficult to construct an instrument that will work well across these varying ability levels.

Still, an accurate assessment of student comprehension ability is both desirable and necessary. Taken individually, assessments pinpoint particular areas of strength and weakness that students can address on their own. Taken collectively, they can provide useful data for curriculum design.

An assessment is said to be valid when it is shown to measure what it claims to measure. As comprehension is fundamental to communication, for an assessment of comprehension to be valid, it should account for the linguistic, sociolinguistic, and discourse features of what is commonly referred to as communicative competence. Canale and Swain (1980) offer an extensive discussion of communicative competence.

Although it is not the purpose of this chapter to provide an inventory of these features or even to describe them in much detail, a brief review is useful here.

Features of linguistic, or grammatical competence may include the following:

• Knowledge of *phonology* and *morphology* (how words/signs are formed)

- *Grammar* (understanding how words/signs work together)
- *Syntax* (the rules that determine how sentences may be constructed)
- *Semantics* (the study of meaning in language).

Sociolinguistic features may include the following:

- Language (dialects, regional variation, personal styles)
- *Register* (the adjustment of language use according to the setting and the role of the participants)
- *Gender* (the dynamics of female and male styles of speech)
- *Contextual* factors (topic, situation, norms of interaction).

Discourse considerations may include the following:

- *Speech acts* (the functions performed by language, e.g., requesting, apologizing, explaining)
- *Background knowledge* (our experience of how the world works helps us interpret meanings)
- *Cohesion* (the links that show connections within discourse)
- *Conversation analysis* (how participants in a conversation produce intelligible utterances and how they interpret the utterances of others).

Again, this is not a comprehensive list of all possible categories and items. Rather, it is a selection from the many features that can profitably be studied and analyzed by students with the goal of improving awareness about how languages work. It is also important to mention that these are not necessarily discrete features. They are in many cases overlapping processes that function simultaneously within discourse.

The list serves, however, as a rough catalogue of structures in language. Starting with phonology as a foundation and developing through phrases, sentences, texts, and context, this is very much the stuff of language—and of interpreting. If communication is the medium and language the mode, these are our materials.

IMMEDIATE RECALL PROTOCOLS

Immediate recall protocols are useful in the development of students' metacognitive skills. Recalls can be used initially to introduce discourse features and to show samples and variations of these selected features. Once students are familiar with the process, recalls can be used to assess student comprehension. These assessments can be used individually to focus on student strengths and weaknesses and collectively to develop curricular materials and lesson plans that are directed toward the identified needs of the students.

Recalls should be introduced to students in sequential order. In general, it is preferable that interpreting students do recalls of spoken English before they attempt recalls of signing. By building a foundation in their L1, students will be better able to perform this exercise in their L2. This offers the additional benefit of observing student proficiency in English. Especially at the community college level where many interpreter education programs are housed, it is rare to find students who do not need some remediation in English. Recalls can provide very accurate information about student competencies.

The Immediate Recall Protocol Procedure

The recall protocol procedure involves the following steps, which have been adapted from Bernhardt's (1991, 187–88) description:

- Select and prepare a text (45–60 seconds of signing or speech).
- Tell students they may hear/see the text as often as they like and that, when they are finished, you will ask them to write down everything they remember from the text.
- Give the students sufficient time to see/hear the text several times.
- Ask the students to look away from the screen and write down everything they remember in English.
- Collect the protocols written by the students.

Use these student-generated data as the basis for future lesson plans that address (1) cultural features, (2) conceptual features, and (3) grammatical features that seem to interfere with comprehension.

Recalls can be conducted in and across different media, intralingually or interlingually: spoken English to spoken English, spoken English to written English, sign to sign, spoken English to sign, and so on. The recall protocol that we review here is of a signed text that was recalled in written English. I chose the written form because it is most congruent with the medium of this presentation. The interlingual form was selected because of its focus on second language comprehension.

Selecting and Preparing a Text

Selecting and preparing the text is probably the most complex and time-consuming part of this process. The text must be at an appropriate level and should be selected in keeping with the knowledge base of the students. At issue here is the way students process individual units of language. As the following examples of student recalls illustrate, students can sometimes handle units of language without comprehending the whole of the text. Students can also reach remarkable, global understandings without being able to handle significant chunks of the text. The recall instrument is especially useful because it can isolate and illuminate these phenomena.

Preparing the text involves both writing a master translation and glossing and categorizing the discourse features of the source material. Two sample glosses are included here. The first is a gloss at the discourse level, which accounts for the discourse function of each utterance (see Figure 1). The second gloss is at the lexical level (see Figure 2). It categorizes each sign by part of speech/part of sentence. The glosses can be used individually to show how language works or in combination to focus on individual items that are problematic for students. The style of gloss is a matter of personal preference. Obviously, the sample text could be glossed and translated in a number of different ways.

Another issue is the length of the chunks. They should be no longer than 45–60 seconds. Typically, a monologue of 3–4 minutes is divided into four or five chunks. The sample shown, "Name Change," is taken from the videotape *ASL Monologues '91*, produced by Gallaudet University. The signer is a young African American woman telling a story about how her name sign changed several times as she moved from school to school early in her teaching career. The monologue is approximately 4 minutes long. For the purpose of the recall, the video was divided into six separate chunks, each approximately 45 seconds in length. Students generally require at least one chunk, sometimes more, to acclimate to the sign style of the model. For this reason, the first couple of chunks are considered a "warm-up" activity. The sample shown here is from the fifth of the six chunks. To show the scope and detail of information available from this procedure in the limited space of this chapter, the sample is limited to just that one "paragraph."

Experiencing the Text

Steps 2, 3, and 4 suggest that the students be allowed to view/hear the source as often as they like. This is recommended for an introduction to the procedure. By allowing students to determine how often they need to see the material, issues of memory and retention are avoided. It also reduces the pressure of performance and allows the student to focus on communicative competence. For more experienced or higher-level students, the teacher may wish to limit the number of viewings, to be agreed on before the procedure starts.

Student-Generated Data

The glosses shown are line-numbered. This allows for easy cross-referencing of the discourse items. In this way the teacher and the students can discover patterns of comprehension—which features are routinely understood, which are troublesome, why some are clear and others not. Once this is known, individual lesson plans offer students an opportunity to work on particularly problematic structures. Structures and features that are difficult for the majority of the class can be highlighted in lesson plans for future classes. In that recalls provide both individual and group diagnostic information, they are doubly useful to the classroom teacher. In that recalls work from student-generated data, they are more personally relevant to the students.

A Sample Recall Protocol Procedure

Sample instruction of the procedure is reviewed in this section. First you will see a master translation of the videotext, followed by three sample student recalls, taken from an Interpreting 1 class. After the student samples, you will see the two glosses described earlier, first the discourse gloss and then the lexical gloss. A group assessment of the student samples is followed by individual assessments of each of the student samples.

MASTER TRANSLATION OF PARAGRAPH 5 FROM "NAME CHANGE"

Then I moved back here and took up my old name sign again. I was working with adults now, so it (the name sign) shouldn't be a problem. But, very interesting, now when students come running up to me and call me "Ruth," I know they're from New Jersey, they're easy to identify. I'll say, "New Jersey?" and they'll say "Right, you remember?" and I'll say, "Yeah." Or if they call me "Sandy" I'll say, "Fanwood" or "Pennsylvania." It's easy because of the different name signs I've had at each of the different schools, Florida, New Jersey, Fanwood, and Pennsylvania.

SAMPLE STUDENT RECALLS

1. Then I moved here. Often I'll meet different people who may know me by my old sign-names. It's very easy for me to quickly recognize them because of the name sign they use to refer to me. Remember I've had four different name signs for each of the four schools I've been to. Now it's very easy to remember them because I remember which school I was in at the time.

2. Then I moved here. I asked if I could go back to my original sign name. They said it was no problem we're all adults. So now when people approach me— use my name sign—it's easy to identify them. I was at four schools with different name signs. Florida, New Jersey, Pennsylvania, now Gallaudet.

3. Then I moved here. I had to go back to using my old sign name, even though I was an adult. But it was very interesting. I would have friends come up to me and sign my old name sign, and I would re-

Text	Discourse Feature/Function in Text
THEN I MOVE-TO HERE	Time marker/Theme/New information
I BACK #T-O OLD<S-CROOK-OF-ELBOW>(name sign)	Cohesion reference/Personal/Comparative
THEY ADULT (initialized)	Cohesion reference/Personal
SHOULD #N-O PROBLEM	Cohesion substitution/Clausal
AND, VERY INTERESTING	Conjunction additive/Topic marker
EVERY TIME STUDENT	Theme/New information
SCL:1 <run-to-me> / BCL: <face excited>	Substitution/Nominal
INDEX-<YOU>	Direct address/Reference/Personal
RUTH (name sign)	Direct address/Given information
I KNOW WHERE FROM	Theme/New information
NJ	Rheme/Given information
EASY IDENTIFY	Theme/New information
I SAY	Direct address/Reference/Personal
YOU NJ	Direct address/Ellipsis/Nominal
<THEY>: YES REMEMBER?	Direct address/New information
<ME:> YES	Direct address/New information
OR SANDY (name sign)	Direct address/Given information
YOU FANWOOD	Direct address/Given information
#O-R – #P-A	Conjunction additive/Given information
EASY	Reiteration/Repetition
YOU KNOW <MY-4> FOUR SCHOOLS	Theme/Given information
#F-L-A	Rheme/Given information
#N-J	Rheme/Given information
DEAF-SCHOOL NEW YORK	Rheme/Given information
#P-A	Rheme/Given information

ure 1. Sample Discourse Gloss

member when and where I met them. (It was easy to identify them.) They would come up to me, "hey, Rich!" I could then tell where I had met people by the name sign they used. If they used the "S" by the side of their face I would know I had met them in NY or in PA. Because I had taught at four different schools, it was easy. I had taught in Florida, Georgia, New York, and Pennsylvania.

Sample Class Analysis

Scoring the recalls involves marking the line number from the discourse gloss of each item that the student text accounts for. Putting

ASL Text	Part of Speech/Sentence Text	
1. THEN	Adverb/Phrasal	
2. I	Noun/Subject	Topic
3. MOVE-TO	Directional Verb/Predicate	
4. HERE	Noun/Object	
5. I	Pronoun/Subject	
6. B-A-C-K	Verb (fs loan sign)/Predicate	
7. #T-O	Preposition (fs)/Phrasal	Comment
8. OLD	Adjective/Phrasal	
9. <"S-crook-of-elbow>(name sign)	Proper Noun/Object	
10. THEY	Pronoun/Subject	Sub-Topic
11. ADULT (initialized)	Adjective/Modifier	
12. SHOULD	Verb/Predicate	
13. #N-O	Adjective/Modifier	Comment
14. PROBLEM	Noun/Object	
15. AND	Conjunction	
16. VERY	Adverb/Modifier	Topic
17. INTERESTING	Noun/Subject	
18. EVERY	Adjective/Modifier	
19. TIME	Noun/Phrasal	Comment
20. STUDENT	Noun/Clause	
21. SCL:1 <run-to-me> BCL	Verb/Predicate Classifier	
22. INDEX-<YOU>	Pronoun/Interrogative	Sub-topic
23. RUTH	Proper Noun	
24. I	Pronoun/Clause	
25. KNOW	Verb/Clause	
26. WHERE	Adjective/Clause	
27. FROM	Preposition/Clause	
28. NJ	Proper Noun/Clause	Comment
29. EASY	Adverb/Clause	
30. IDENTIFY	Verb/Clause	
31. I	Pronoun/Clause	
32. SAY	Verb/Clause	
33. YOU	Pronoun/Clause	Sub-topic
34. NJ	Proper Noun/Clause	

Figure 2. Sample Lexical Gloss

ASL Text	Part of Speech/Sentence Text	
35. <THEY:> YES	Adverb/Clause	
36. REMEMBER?	Verb/Clause	Comment
37. <ME:>YES	Adverb/Clause	
38. OR	Conjunction	Sub-topic
39. SANDY (name sign)	Proper Noun/Subject	
40. YOU	Pronoun/Clause	Comment
41. FANWOOD	Proper Noun/Clause	
42. #O-R	Conjunction (fs)	Sub-topic
43. #P-A	Proper Noun/Clause	Comment
44. EASY	Adverb/Predicate	
45. <YOU>	Pronoun/Subject	
46. KNOW	Verb/Predicate	
47. <MY-4>	Pronoun/Modifier	Topic
48. FOUR	Adjective/Modifier	
49. SCHOOLS	Noun/Object	
50. #F-L-A	Proper Noun (fs)/Object	
51. #N-J	Proper Noun (fs)/Object	
52. DEAF-SCHOOL	Noun/Object	Comment
53. NEW YORK (mouths "FANWOOD")	Proper Noun/Object	
54. #P-A	Proper Noun (fs)/Object	

Figure 2. *Continued*

the line number in parentheses indicates information from the gloss that is misinterpreted. Using this method on the preceding student samples yields the following results (numbers correspond to lines in the sample discourse gloss):

Student #1: 1, (7), 12, 21, 20

Student #2: 1, (2), (3), 7, 9, 10, 12, 21, 22, 23, 25, (24)

Student #3: 1, (2), (3), 5, 6, 7, 16, 8, (9), 10, 12, 17, 18, 19, 20, 21, 22, (23), 24, 25

On closer inspection, items 1, 12, and 21 were accounted for in some form in each of the student recalls. Each of these is listed as a "theme" in the gloss. Items 2, 3, 4, 11, 13, 14, 15, and 16, which represent forms of cohesion, rheme, and direct address, were not interpreted accurately in any of the recalls. This is significant information from the standpoint of curriculum development. Items that were not accounted for and the structures they exemplify can be targeted for classroom instruction.

As mentioned, the gloss shows that items 1, 12, and 21 are all thematic elements in the discourse. Theme is a grammatical category of the arrangement of information in a sentence. The theme refers to the central element of the sentence; the information around which the sentence is built. Note that lines 11 and 22–25 are designated as "rhemes." Rhemes are those items in a discourse that follow and amplify the theme. Halliday (1994) provides a comprehensive review of theme, rheme, and other categories of discourse feature. Once the concept of theme and rheme is introduced, ask students to describe the relationship between it and the topic/comment structure frequently seen in ASL syntax.

In this example none of the students could identify that the reason Sandy reassumed her previous name sign was that she was now working with adults (lines 2–4). From the gloss we can see that these items are all forms of cohesion, that is, words or phrases that establish relationships between sentences or utterances. What is the missing link here for students? Why were they unable to render an accurate meaning for this stretch? Often the best way to proceed with this is to replay the video and ask the students directly. The purpose of this sort of inquiry is not necessarily to uncover the students' mental processes but to allow the students to discover individually how information is structured in a language. Elements of cohesion are often called text-forming devices. Why would they be called this, and how do they form a text? By comparing the lexical gloss to the discourse gloss, can you see how these elements relate to one another and to the sentences and utterances they create?

The students also had difficulty with lines 13–16, which no one accounted for. A check of the gloss shows that these are all forms of direct address, or "reported speech." This ASL feature often confuses students. The pronominal references are often too subtle for students to catch. They are left with a vague understanding of what was said but not of who said it or to whom. In this instance, the video might be replayed in slow motion so that the students can catch the references they missed. Once they have identified these references, have the students bring to the next class different video samples that show similar pronominal referencing. By allowing the students to reinforce their learning with examples of their own, this new information moves from the realm of scholastic knowledge to personal knowledge, a crucial distinction in the learning process.

Note that these students did well with a unique construction. On line 21, the subject signs "YOU-KNOW" with her right hand and then makes the sign "4" with her left, slightly inflecting the "4" to point toward herself with her fingertips (<MY-4>) and then bringing the "4" out to become a base hand for a list of four items. The transformation of the "4" from personal pronoun to reference point is unusual. Still, each of the students was able to make a meaningful translation of it. It is interesting to ask students how they came to these meanings. In some cases they can offer plausible reasons, but often they cannot. A discussion on the concept of tacit knowledge of a language can be very effective in this circumstance.

Once students are familiar with the recall protocol procedure, they are assigned to devise one of their own. From any signed video-text available, they create both a gloss and a master translation and then present these to the class. The discoveries students make in doing this work, both individually and collectively, provide marvelous opportunities for learning. Discussions on categorizing are especially enlightening as they reinforce the multiplicity of choices that bear on successful interpreting.

Sample Individual Analysis

The student recalls, their scoring, and individual comments on the status of their work are reprinted in the following section.

1. Then I moved here. Often I'll meet different people who may know me by my old sign-names. It's very easy for me to quickly recognize them because of the name sign they use to refer to me. Remember I've had 4 different name signs for each of the four schools I've been to. Now, it's very easy to remember them because I remember which school I was in at the time.

Scoring: 1, (7), 12, 21, 20

This student is unable to account for a sizable portion of the text. None of the fingerspelling was recorded, nor were any of the specific pronominal references. The virtue of the recall procedure in this case is that it affords very specific information on the extent and particulars of a student's lack of awareness. Instead of saying, "You missed a lot of information," the teacher can point to the variety of structures and features that the student missed. This student does manage to provide a reasonably good summary of the text. It might be useful in this case to explore the differences between summarizing and interpreting. At the very least, this student is in serious need of remediation in sign comprehension skills.

2. Then I moved here. I asked if I could go back to my original sign name. They said it was no problem we're all adults. So now when people approach me — use my name sign it's easy to identify them. I was at four schools with different name signs. Florida, New Jersey, Pennsylvania — now Gallaudet.

Scoring: 1, (2), (3), 7, 9, 10, 12, 21, 22, 23, 25, (24)

Student #2 details roughly half of the information, but this, too, is more of a summary than a translation. The three instances of misinterpretation are obvious topics for discussion. In addition, this rendering is almost without attention to affect. The speaker used a great deal of facial inflection and exuded a warm, almost bubbly, personality. That none of this survived the translation by #2 is significant.

3. Then I moved here. I had to go back to using my old sign name, even though I was an adult. But it was very interesting. I would have friends come up to me and sign my old name sign and I would remember when and where I met them. (It was easy to identify them.) They would come up to me, "hey, Rich!" I could then tell where I had met people by the name sign they used. If they used the "S" by the side of their face I would know I had met them in NY or in PA. Because I had taught at 4 different schools it was easy. I had taught in Florida, Georgia, New York and Pennsylvania.

Scoring: 1, (2), (3), 5, 6, 7, 16, 8, (9), 10, 12, 17, 18, 19, 20, 21, 22, (23), 24, 25

This student does a reasonably good job of capturing both content and affect of the text. Of particular interest here is the utterance

"Hey, Rich!" in reference to the speaker, who is a woman. The name Rich appears nowhere in the text of the speaker. Was it a mistake in writing? How can the student account for this anomaly?

It is often useful to review these recalls with students individually for the purpose of such clarifications. When asked where that interpretation came from, the student had no idea. This presents an opportunity to discuss metacognition and other forms of strategic competence. How do we know what we know? What do we know about what we know? What techniques can be employed to monitor output on a conscious level? This individualized analysis of meta-cognitive ability can be a productive learning experience for students and teachers.

SUMMARY

Metacognition and strategic competence are of great interest in interpreter training. Interpreters make strategic decisions on a continuous basis as they negotiate meaning between languages. They are constantly employing all conceivable aspects of their capability to receive, process, and produce information. Strategic competence, the ability to cope with the quirks of authentic language usage, is an ability that interpreters cannot do without. Following the conception that comprehension drives production in language learning as well as interpreting, the significance of strategic competence comes to light. Error repair, clarification strategies, and maintaining clear communication without complete information are all part of the moment-to-moment experience of interpreting.

Recognition of differences between learners, in cognitive style, in aptitude, attitude, and motivation has wrought remarkable change in classrooms. As the field of interpreter education continues to evolve, it will necessarily connect with other, as yet untapped, domains of knowledge. I have here offered second language reading comprehension as one such domain. Focusing on comprehension as the essential element in language proficiency means reassessing not only how receptive skills are taught and learned but also how they are evaluated. Immediate recall protocols offer a heuristic that allows students and instructors to inquire into the current state of their competencies and to diagnose strengths and weaknesses on an individual basis.

The trend toward individuation, in the construction of meaning, in the delivery of instruction, and in the assessment of learning carries with it the need for flexibility in teaching and testing. Classroom teachers can use recalls to isolate curricular needs and to measure curricular results and the thought processes that underlie comprehension.

REFERENCES

Agar, M. 1994. *Language shock.* New York: Quill.

Bartley, D. 1970. The importance of the attitude factor in language dropout: A preliminary investigation of group and sex differences. *Foreign Language Annals* 3 (3): 383–93.

Bernhardt, E. 1991. *Reading development in a second language.* Norwood, N.J.: Ablex.

Bloome, D., P. Puro, and E. Theodorou. 1989. Procedural display and classroom lessons. *Curriculum Inquiry* 19 (3): 265–91.

Canale, M., and M. Swain. 1980. Theoretical bases of communicative approaches to second language teaching and testing. *Applied Linguistics* 1:1–47.

Christison, M., and K. Krahnke. 1986. Student perceptions of academic language study. *TESOL Quarterly* 20 (1): 61–79.

Cohen, A. 1977. Successful second language speakers: A review of research literature. *Journal for the Israel Association of Applied Linguistics.* ERIC Document Reproduction Service No. ED 142 085.

Cook, G. 1989. *Discourse.* Oxford: Oxford University Press.

de Jong, D., and Stevenson, D., eds. 1990. *Individualizing the assessment of language abilities.* Clevendon: Multilingual Matters.

Halliday, M. A. K. 1994. *An introduction to functional grammar.* 2d ed. London: Edward Arnold.

Horowitz, R. Discourse organization in oral and written language: Critical contrasts for literacy and schooling. In *Individualizing the assessment of language abilities,* ed. D. de Jong and D. Stevenson. Clevendon: Multilingual Matters.

Jacobs, R. 1996. Just how hard is it to learn ASL? The case for ASL as a truly foreign language. In *Multicultural aspects of sociolinguistics in Deaf communities,* ed. C. Lucas. Washington, D.C.: Gallaudet University Press.

Mantle–Bromley, C. 1995. Positive attitudes and realistic beliefs: Links to proficiency. *The Modern Language Journal* 79 (3): 372–86.

National Center for Education Statistics. 1994. *NAEP 1992 writing report card.* Washington, D.C.: Office of Educational Research and Improvement.

Nunan, D. 1989. *Designing tasks for the communicative classroom.* Cambridge: Cambridge University Press.

———. 1993. *Introducing discourse analysis.* London: Penguin Books.

Oxford, R., and J. Shearin. 1994. Language learning motivation: Expanding the theoretical framework. *The Modern Language Journal* 78 (1): 12–28.

Ramage, K. 1990. Motivational factors and persistence in foreign language study. *Language Learning* 40 (2): 189–219.

Reddy, M. 1979. The conduit metaphor: A case of frame conflict in our language about language. In *Metaphor and thought,* ed. A. Ortony. Cambridge: Cambridge University Press.

Reinert, H. 1970. Student attitudes toward foreign language: No sale! *The Modern Language Journal* 55 (2): 107–12.

Roberts, L. 1992. Attitudes of entering university freshmen toward foreign language study: A descriptive analysis. *The Modern Language Journal* 76 (3): 275–83.

Schiffrin, D. 1994. *Approaches to discourse.* Cambridge, Mass.: Blackwell.

Stanovich, K. 1980. Toward an interactive-compensatory model of individual differences in the development of reading fluency. *Reading Research Quarterly* 16:32–71.

Van Lier, L. 1995. *Introducing language awareness.* London: Penguin Books.

Whitney, P., and D. Budd. 1996. Think-aloud protocols and the study of comprehension. *Discourse Processes* 21 (3): 341–51.

APPENDIX 1
Suggested Readings

Language Awareness

Hawkins, E. 1984. *Awareness of language: An introduction*. Cambridge: Cambridge University Press.

Van Lier, L. 1995. *Introducing language awareness*. London: Penguin Books.

Discourse Analysis

Halliday, M. A. K. 1985. *An introduction to functional grammar*. London: Edward Arnold.

Halliday, M. A. K., and R. Hasan. 1976. *Cohesion in English*. London: Longman.

Hatch, E. 1992. *Discourse and language education*. Cambridge: Cambridge University Press.

Nunan, D. 1993. *Introducing discourse analysis*. London: Penguin Books.

Schiffrin, D. 1994. *Approaches to discourse*. Cambridge, Mass.: Blackwell.

Second-Language Reading Comprehension

Bernhardt, E. 1991. *Reading development in a second language: Theoretical, empirical, and classroom perspectives*. Norwood, N.J.: Ablex.

JANICE H. HUMPHREY

Portfolios

One Answer to the Challenge of Assessment and the "Readiness to Work" Gap

PORTFOLIOS ORIGINATED in the fine arts as a collection of artifacts to demonstrate one's best works or accomplishments as well as the range of one's ability, skill, or knowledge. They are now used in a number of fields, especially in writing (Belanoff and Dickson 1991), in a variety of ways. One is an educational *assessment portfolio* in which a student compiles various documents that demonstrate mastery of identified skills and/or knowledge laid out by a standard or criterion. In this adaptation, this documentation would consist of items such as samples of written work, audiotapes and/or videotapes, letters, and awards.

In the Program of Sign Language Interpretation at Douglas College in British Columbia, we use a *graduation portfolio* to determine a student's mastery of program outcomes in order to qualify for graduation.[1] In the graduation portfolio, students compile written and videotaped evidence to demonstrate readiness to enter the field of ASL/English interpretation. Documents may include graded work from courses taken in the interpreting program, papers and videotapes developed specifically for the portfolio, excerpts from students' journals, and letters from professional interpreters and/or clients with whom the students worked during their practicum.

---

1. The portfolio process and requirements have evolved from the work of a number of individuals, including Marna Arnell, Roger Carver, Nigel Howard, Jan Humphrey, Janice Jickels, Karen Malcolm, Barb Mykle–Hotzen, Cheryl Palmer, and Debra Russell.

153

When submitted, portfolios are assessed by a team of three individuals: a faculty member, a professional interpreter, and a member of the Deaf community. Assessors use a scoring form on which they document the types of evidence provided (direct/indirect) and their determination of student mastery in each area and any notes or questions they may have. After reviewing the portfolio, an interview is held between the assessment team and the student. During the interview, assessors ask questions about portfolio contents, solicit additional information in areas with unclear or insufficient evidence, or clarify portfolio documents. Based on the portfolio and interview, the assessment team then recommends the student for graduation or remediation. The team determines what type of remediation is required and sets timelines for the submission of additional or revised portfolio sections. Depending on the team's degree of concern, a student may be required to complete the work assigned within six days, six weeks, or six months. The team reviews the remedial work submitted and reinterviews the student to determine if she or he is now qualified to graduate from the program.

Evolution of Graduation Portfolios at Douglas College

In 1994 our faculty began discussing ways we could verify that our students were ready to work upon graduation.[2] We realized that our grading standards varied from the first to the fourth semester to account for students' evolving mastery of the knowledge and skills they were learning. As a result, we began to question the validity of assigning the same value to grades earned in all four semesters in determining if students were ready to graduate. We reviewed articles from the National Institute for Staff and Organizational Development at the University of Texas that presented various creative approaches to student evaluation. We spent a great deal of time discussing the concept of critical thinking and reflection and made a

---

2. This discussion came about because of issues raised at the 1994 Conference of Interpreter Trainers meeting in Charlotte, N.C.

commitment to encourage students to develop the habit of thinking critically and reflecting on their work. Finally, we looked at the use of portfolios including use by academic institutions to evaluate teaching effectiveness and grant tenure, as well as use by instructors to evaluate student performance.

Knowing that we could not teach students everything in two years, we made a commitment to prepare students with the skills and knowledge required to enter the field and the tools necessary to support professional development and lifelong learning. Further, our faculty determined that it is critical for members of the Deaf community and professional interpreters to verify that our "product" is satisfactory to the consumers.

We began experimenting with a graduation portfolio as a summative evaluation approach to determine student readiness to graduate and enter the field in 1995. All fourth-semester courses are marked on a "mastery/nonmastery" basis. Graduation portfolios are submitted and form the summative basis of evaluation for all courses.

The format has gone through several iterations, and we have settled on a program outcomes base. Looking at the work of successful practitioners, we identified six student outcomes areas (see Figure 1).

Evaluation of Experience to Date

Our overall experience with the graduation portfolio has been quite positive. Assessors are pleased because students submit a three-inch, three-ring binder plus six to eight videotapes that are clearly marked for assessor review. Each section is distinct from the others, so skill-sets are more easily tracked by assessors as they determine whether the student has demonstrated mastery section by section. All materials presented are current, summative samples of the student's work—the interpreting and ASL samples are made three weeks prior to submission of the portfolio and reflect the student's language and interpreting skills at the point of request for graduation.

1. Communicate bilingually	❖ Produce and comprehend grammatically correct, register-variant ASL capable of sustaining near-native dialogues and monologues; ❖ Produce and comprehend grammatically correct, register-variant English capable of sustaining near-native dialogues and monologues; ❖ Identify linguistic features of ASL and English and discuss specific challenges of these differences for interpreters.
2. Act biculturally	❖ Identify rules for social interaction in both the Deaf and hearing communities and discuss the role of hearing people on the Deaf community and related challenges for interpreters; ❖ Demonstrate appropriate attention-getting strategies, turn-taking behaviors, and other rules for social interaction in the Deaf community. Graduates will adapt these appropriately to a range of contexts and settings; ❖ Demonstrate appropriate attention-getting strategies, turn-taking behaviors, and other rules for social interaction in the English-speaking community. Graduates will adapt these appropriately to a range of contexts and settings.
3. Act ethically	❖ Demonstrate a pattern of critical thinking when making and discussing professional decisions; ❖ Discuss power, power structures, and systems within which one may work and the implications for interpreters; ❖ Identify the underlying principles of the Code of Ethics and relevant laws, applying them to professional decisions; ❖ Behave in ways that support and respect diversity; ❖ Act professionally in relationships with consumers, other interpreters, etc. (communicating, problem solving, negotiating, setting boundaries, etc.); ❖ Participate in professional organizations and upgrading, striving toward national certification.

Figure 1. Program Outcomes Criteria

4. Interpret meaning	❖ Take in and analyze linguistic utterances (expressed and implied) and contextual factors to identify essential elements of meaning;
	❖ Produce an utterance in the target language that conveys the original meaning/intent and maintains dynamic equivalence between the individuals engaged in the interaction;
	❖ Monitor work and make corrections as needed;
	❖ Manage the overall interpreting process (e.g., decide on the use of consecutive or simultaneous interpreting, interrupting the speaker if need be, etc.).
5. Take care of self	❖ Manage time effectively;
	❖ Care for self emotionally, physically, spiritually, and nutritionally by setting appropriate personal and professional boundaries/goals;
	❖ Establish support networks and maintain effective interpersonal communication;
	❖ Reflect on personal practice and set future goals.
6. Use effective business practices	❖ Demonstrate effective interpersonal communications, acting respectfully with all people;
	❖ Engage in professional consultations (e.g., with team interpreter, interpreting or Deaf mentor, etc.), including appropriate preparation and debriefing of assignments;
	❖ Present a professional demeanor (appropriate attire and deportment) for various settings;
	❖ Follow field standards related to negotiating fees and contracts, self-marketing, invoicing, and accounting;
	❖ Communicate effectively in standard written business English.

Figure 1. *Continued*

Program faculty have found a new level of accountability as we work side by side with community assessors. Because we work with the students semester after semester, we sometimes confuse our sense of student progress with current performance. More than once, a faculty member has said that a student showed satisfactory skill in an area, only to be challenged by one of the community assessors who brought "fresh eyes" to the project. These dialogues have led to one of the greatest benefits to the program. Members of the Deaf community and professional interpreters know that program faculty respect their input and will not certify a student for graduation until the whole team agrees that the student is ready to graduate. As a result, there is enhanced commitment to students and to the program, evidenced by the willingness of community members to volunteer in a number of ways.

IMPLEMENTATION OF THE GRADUATE PORTFOLIO

Introduction of Graduation Standards to Students

Graduation outcomes are available in our program brochure for review by potential students. Applicants are told about the graduation portfolio during the screening weekend prior to program admission. We want them to know all the program requirements as they select the program they want to enroll in. The expected outcomes are also referred to by instructors in all courses throughout the program, and students begin relating their learning and level of performance to the exiting standards as soon as they begin the program.

Supporting Students in the Development of Portfolios

During the third semester, we incorporate portfolio seminars into our schedule. In these seminars we discuss each competency area in depth and show students samples of successful portfolios. At this time, students are provided with an evidence guide that states required and optional documentation in each outcome area (see Figure 2). We invite program graduates in to share their portfolios and

Communicate Bilingually

Required   ❖ Submit a typed, double-spaced reflective paper (4–6 pages), defining the concept of "communicating bilingually" and give examples of your experiences in this area. Outline specific examples of linguistic difference between English and ASL and give examples of your evolving mastery of each language. Outline your plans for continued linguistic development over the next three to five years.

❖ Complete the Canadian Sign Language Competence Interview at Level VIII or better. Include a copy of your interview results.

❖ Provide two ASL language samples—one in which you give a 5-minute introduction of yourself to the Deaf member of your assessment team; a second showing a 10-minute dialogue between you and your fourth-semester ASL instructor.

❖ Provide a sample of consultative register spoken English (10 minutes in length). You will use your final practicum seminar presentation for this sample.

Optional   ❖ Provide excerpts from class papers or projects demonstrating your mastery of this outcome.

❖ Provide written feedback from practicum supervisors, college instructors, professional interpreters, or consumers, commenting on your abilities in this area.

Act Biculturally

Required   ❖ Submit a typed, double-spaced reflective paper (4–6 pages) defining the concept of "bicultural behavior" and give examples of your experiences in this area. Outline specific examples of cultural differences between mainstream and Deaf cultures and give examples of your evolving mastery of each culture. Outline your plans for continued cultural evolution over the next three to five years.

❖ Provide written feedback from practicum supervisors, college instructors, professional interpreters, or consumers, commenting on your abilities in both mainstream cultural interactions and Deaf cultural interactions.

Optional   ❖ Provide excerpts from class papers, journal entries, or class projects that demonstrate your mastery of this outcome.

Figure 2. Graduation Portfolio Documentation

Interpret Meaning

Required   ❖ Submit a typed, double-spaced reflective paper (4–6 pages) defining the concept of "interpreting meaning" and give examples of your experiences in this area. Outline specific steps in the process of interpreting meaning and give examples to support your statements. Outline your plans for continued skills development in this area over the next three to five years.

❖ Submit one or more videotapes of your interpreting work taken at a practicum site. Complete a self-assessment on the sample.

❖ Submit three videotaped samples of your interpreting work based on stimulus material selected by the program (sign-to-voice; voice-to-sign; interactive). You will receive preparatory material for these assignments one week before you record the tapes. You will interpret with a partner. You may consult any preparatory sources or reference materials you wish. Complete a self-assessment on each tape, commenting on your preparation activities as well as the effectiveness of the teamwork between yourself and your partner.

Optional   ❖ Submit additional videotaped samples of your interpreting work with self-assessment;

❖ Provide written feedback from practicum supervisors, college instructors, professional interpreters, or consumers commenting on your interpreting abilities.

Act Ethically

Required   ❖ Submit a typed, double-spaced reflective paper (4–6 pages) discussing your understanding of professionalism and ethical behavior. Provide examples of your application of this principle to your work as an interpreter. Outline your plans for continued ethical/professional development over the next three to five years, including your action plan leading to AVLIC certification.

❖ Provide letters or written feedback from practicum supervisors, college instructors, professional interpreters, or consumers, commenting on your decision making and actions regarding professional and ethical issues.

❖ Provide proof of membership in WAVLI/AVLIC. Submit a brief paper (2–3 pages) discussing ways you have been/will be involved in WAVLI in the next three years.

Figure 2. *Continued*

Act Ethically (*Continued*)

Optional
- ❖ Provide excerpts from class papers or projects demonstrating your mastery of this outcome.

- ❖ Provide comments from professional interpreters and/or consumers commenting on your ethical and professional choices.

Take Care of Self

Required
- ❖ Submit a typed, double-spaced reflective paper (4–6 pages) detailing your understanding of wellness and self-care. Explain how you have learned to deal with the challenge of wellness in your daily life. Include a statement of personal goals for continued growth in this area, along with an action plan of how you will accomplish these goals.

Optional
- ❖ Provide a copy of your daytimer, clearly showing how you manage your time well. You may submit a simulated schedule or change identifying details as appropriate.

Use Appropriate Business Skills

Required
- ❖ Submit a typed, double-spaced reflective paper (4–6 pages) detailing what "appropriate business skills" means to you, providing examples of your use of these in your daily practice. Include a statement of personal goals for continued growth in this area over the next three to five years.

- ❖ Provide samples of an invoice and details of the accounting system you will use for freelance work upon graduation. Include a statement of self-marketing strategies and tools you plan to use to start your freelance business.

- ❖ Provide a cover letter and résumé applying for the type of job you plan to target upon graduation. Include a list of agencies, school districts, and so on where you plan to apply for work and explain why you are interested in working in the selected area.

Optional
- ❖ Provide letters or written feedback from practicum supervisors, college instructors, professional interpreters, or consumers, commenting on your abilities.

Figure 2. *Continued*

discuss their experiences in its development. Students are required to submit drafts of reflection papers in order to receive feedback regarding the content and clarity of their writing four months before portfolios are to be submitted.

PORTFOLIO EVIDENCE GUIDE

Assessing the Portfolios

Prior to submission of portfolios, the program coordinator sets up assessment teams and assigns three or four students to each team. On the day portfolios are submitted, all evaluators meet to review program standards, refresh memories regarding types of evidence, and actually evaluate one or two portfolios together. This ensures interrater reliability (see the scoring form in Appendix 1). Each evaluation team determines its approach to the task. Some teams choose to mark the portfolio together; others mark them independently and then come together to compare observations. Ultimately the team must decide unanimously whether the student satisfies program standards for graduation based upon the portfolio.

In reviewing portfolios, assessors are looking for evidence that a student can perform at a level necessary to begin work as an interpreter. This is an important point. Assessors are aware that students are on the cusp of graduation. With this in mind, assessors are not looking for perfection. Rather, they are looking for the following characteristics:

- Demonstration of emerging language, culture, and interpreting knowledge and skills
- Ability to reflect and synthesize learning
- Ability to self-assess interpreting work, interpersonal interactions, their emerging professional identity and values base, and decisions
- Use of professional language and ability to articulate professional standards
- Professional behavior, decision making, and demeanor
- Understanding of the field, plan for self-marketing, and commitment to lifelong professional development.

Recommendation Options

An evaluation team can make one of several decisions:

1. They may deem the student successful in all sections of the portfolio. In this event, they meet with the student to ask any clarifying questions they may have, encourage the student, and personally confirm that the faculty and representatives from the interpreting and Deaf communities believe they are ready to graduate.

2. They may deem the student mostly successful but not up to the standard in some areas. In this case, the interview takes on greater importance. If the student can convince the evaluators that she or he does have the knowledge or skill-set in question, the team can conclude that the student is ready to graduate. However, if the student is unable to clarify questions or demonstrate the knowledge/skills in question, the evaluators may send the student away with the portfolio to rework particular areas. In this event, a timeline and follow-up interview will be scheduled within two weeks to allow the student to graduate with her or his class. After reviewing the improved portfolio and conducting the second interview, evaluators determine whether the student is ready to graduate. Recommendations are made to the program coordinator regarding additional work required of this student.

3. They may deem the student's portfolio mostly unsuccessful. In this case, they usually return the portfolio and allow the student six months to work on it. After reviewing the improved portfolio and conducting the second interview, evaluators again determine whether the student is ready to graduate. Recommendations are made to the program coordinator regarding additional work required of this student.

Sample Case Studies

Student A submits her portfolio. Evaluators find it to be comprehensive, meeting program standards. They are satisfied that the student has the language and interpreting skills necessary to begin work as an interpreter. They have some questions of a minor nature to ask the student, as well as some suggestions and comments to make to the student during the portfolio interview, but they generally agree that this student is ready to graduate. In this case, the interview is fairly short and focused. Assessment team members ask their questions, make comments on particular sections of the portfolio, confirm the student's job search plans, and compliment the student on her progress to date. They confirm recommendation for graduation and welcome the student as a new interpreter in the field.

Student B submits his portfolio. Assessors find it to be comprehensive and up to program standards in five of six sections. However, they are somewhat concerned about the area of interpretation. In the videotapes submitted, some successful samples of interpretation are shown—examples of conveying meaning between English and ASL, making appropriate linguistic and cultural adaptations. The videotapes also show some unsuccessful samples in which source language meaning is not conveyed in the target language. However, the assessors are not convinced that the student can analyze his work, delineating between successful and unsuccessful work, identifying errors, patterns, and strategies to resolve concerns. The team asks the student to view one of the interpreting tapes during the portfolio interview and to demonstrate the ability to analyze the work correctly. In this case, the student analyzes the work to the satisfaction of the assessment team. The interview continues, during which team members ask clarifying questions, make comments to the student regarding future plans, and so on. Because the team is satisfied that this student is ready to enter the field, they tell the student he will be recommended for graduation. In the event the student is unable to satisfy team members, they will ask the student to resubmit one or more self-assessment documents for the interpreting samples within a certain period of time. If the resubmitted work meets program standards, the student will be approved to graduate. If not, the student will be given an "incomplete" in all fourth-semester courses and placed on a learning contract, typically six months in length (see the sample contract in Appendix 2). When the remedial work is completed, the work is resubmitted to the evaluation team to determine readiness to graduate.

Student C hands in her portfolio, which seems carelessly put together. Written work lacks depth, clarity, and evidence of reflection.

The critique of interpreting samples is skimpy and does not indicate that the student can determine whether her work is successful. The evaluation team returns the portfolio to the student unmarked, requiring the student to redo the whole thing and submit it within ten days. When resubmitted, some areas of the portfolio are considered "up to standard," but other sections are still lacking. The team is concerned with (a) the student's inability to analyze interpretation accurately; (b) a lack of evidence that the student is able to interact appropriately with members of the Deaf community; and (c) the student's ASL skills. The team meets with the student and asks clarifying questions on the sections deemed up to par. They then explain their concerns about the remaining sections of the portfolio and outline an independent contract. The student is required to do the following:

1. Interpret three videotapes—one in July, one in August, and one in September—and complete an analysis of each. The July and August tapes are to be done with a colleague or mentor, and the student's goals are to identify successful/unsuccessful work, explain why each sample is/is not successful, identify errors and patterns, and outline strategies to resolve concerns. The September tape is to be submitted to the assessment team to replace work submitted in the original portfolio.

2. Contact a specific Deaf individual from the final practicum site and ask that person to contact the Deaf community member of the assessment team by e-mail to confirm the student's appropriateness when interacting with the Deaf community. This is to be completed by July 1.

3. Attend fifteen hours of Deaf community events between May and September, submitting a log of interactions in September. The student must provide evidence that interactions included a range of ages, settings, and degree of formality.

4. Retake the ASL interview and provide evidence of ASL skills at Level VIII by September 1.

The student contacts program personnel in late August and indicates that she has had difficulty completing the community hours due to conflicts in her summer working schedule and community interaction opportunities. Further, the student has been unable to retake the ASL interview because the administering body has not been available in the summer months. A one-month extension is awarded. When the work is resubmitted, the team assesses it. They are satisfied with the quality and depth of all four requirements. They reinterview the student, ask some clarifying questions, verify job search plans, and confer recommendation for graduation.

SERENDIPITOUS BENEFITS

Clearly stated program outcomes inform prospective students of the program's expectations for a graduate. In addition, the portfolio gives us a holistic, integrated way to assess student readiness to graduate and enter the field of ASL/English interpretation. Several other benefits accrue as well.

Student Benefits

The first and greatest benefit of the graduation portfolio is to students. They graduate from our program with a clear sense that they are ready to work. They leave the program with samples of their work, the ability to discuss decisions they make, and the ability to work effectively with colleagues in the field. According to Malcolm (1996, 49–50), other benefits include the following:

1. Students consistently report having a strong sense of their own achievement through the development of the portfolio. Rather than relying on an instructor's assessment of their abilities and limitations, they report a confidence in their own judgment. They also report feeling pleasantly surprised at the amount they *do* know.

2. Students also state that materials they develop for the portfolio are directly useful in their job search. Résumés, business cards, and invoice forms as well as video samples of interpreting skills are immediately available for presentation. In addition, the degree of reflection required to assemble the portfolio prepares students to quickly respond to questions regarding their strengths and limitations, their understanding of cross-cultural communication, and their understanding of current issues in the field. Awareness of their

limitations also guides them in accepting or declining work and in preparing their own professional development plans.

3. Students feel validated by the community members' "stamp of approval" as opposed to being assessed solely by faculty members. This increases their confidence as they shed their student status and take their first tentative steps into the world of professional interpreting.

4. Finally, the cumulative nature of the portfolio encourages students to see the interconnectedness of their learning.

Relationship with Employers

The graduation portfolio allows us to verify student readiness to work. At a recent advisory committee meeting, one employer impressed upon the faculty the importance of this benefit. The committee was discussing the critical shortage of interpreters and steps the program could take to address the issue. This employer—who would not employ graduates from our program seven years ago—said, "Whatever you do to address the interpreter shortage, do not lower your standards. Employers have come to trust that Douglas College graduates are really able to do the job. Don't do anything to change that."

Relationship with the Community

The faculty respects the recommendations and decisions of the assessment team. This has had a powerful impact on our relationship with the community. They know we listen to them and that they have a voice in determining when a student is ready to work. As a result, their commitment to the program and to the students is very strong. Professional interpreters accept a first-year student as a "twin" to provide individual support and encouragement during the student's first year. Deaf community members volunteer to work with students in a variety of ways—as talent in interpreting role-plays, as tutors and culture guides, and so on. This has strengthened the program in many ways.

Program Evaluation and Curriculum Review

Finally, generation of a comprehensive list of skill and knowledge sets required for a beginning interpreter allows us to review our curriculum to verify that we are in fact teaching those skills and knowledge sets. It also allows us to identify knowledge or skills that we teach in our curriculum but did not include in our list, challenging us to ask whether these are essential areas of instruction. The graduation portfolio also provides a wonderful approach to program evaluation. If students are consistently weak in a particular skill or knowledge set, we know we need to return to our curriculum, identify that particular skill/knowledge set, and modify our approach to instruction. It also helps us reduce overlap and ambiguity.

REFERENCES AND RESOURCES

Angelo, T., and K. P. Cross. 1993. *Classroom assessment techniques: A hand-book for college teachers.* 2d ed. San Francisco: Jossey-Bass.

Belanoff, P., and M. Dickson, eds. 1991. *Portfolios: Process and product.* Portsmouth, N.H.: Heinemann.

Carr, C., and Kemmis, S. 1983. *Becoming critical: Knowing through action research.* Victoria, Australia: Deakin University Press.

Carter, R. E. 1984. *Dimensions of moral education.* Toronto: University of Toronto Press.

Clandinin, J. 1986. *Classroom practice: Teacher images in action.* Philadelphia: Falmer Press.

Connelly, F. M., and Clandinin, J. 1985. Personal practical knowledge and the modes of knowing: Relevance for teaching and learning. In *Learning and teaching the ways of knowing,* ed. E. Eisner. Chicago: University of Chicago Press.

Donmoyer, R. 1985. *How we think: A restatement of the relation of reflective thinking to the educative process.* Chicago: D.C. Heath.

Edgerton, R., P. Hutchings, and K. Quinlan. 1991. *The teaching portfolio: Capturing the scholarship in teaching.* Washington, D.C.: American Association for Higher Education.

Elbaz, F. 1983. *Teacher thinking: A study of practical knowledge.* London: Croom Helm.

Grimmett, P. O., T. J. Riecken, A. M. MacKinnon, and G. L. Erickson. 1987. Studying reflective practice: A review of research. Paper presented at the Working Conference on Reflective Teaching, University of Houston, Texas, October 8-11.

Malcolm, K. 1996. Assessing exiting competencies: A portfolio approach. In *Proceedings of the Eleventh National Convention,* Conference of Interpreter Trainers, ed. D. Jones. Little Rock, Arkansas.

Portfolio use in higher education: A primer. *The Beacon* 8, no. 5. St. Norbert College.

Schon, D. A. 1983. *The reflective practitioner: How professionals think in action.* New York: Basic Books.

———. 1987. *Educating the reflective practitioner: Toward a new design for teaching and learning in the professions.* San Francisco: Jossey-Bass.

Schulman, L. 1994. *Toward a pedagogy of cases: Case methods in teacher education,* ed. J. Schulman. New York: Teachers College Press.

Shore, B. M., et al. 1986. *The teaching dossier: A guide to its preparation and use,* rev. ed. Montreal: Canadian Association of University Teachers.

The portfolio process and accountability. *Innovation Abstracts* 15, no. 12. University of Texas: National Institute for Staff and Organizational Development.

Van Mann, M. 1977. Linking ways of knowing with ways of being practical. *Curriculum Inquiry* 6 (3): 205–28.

Vavrus, L., and A. Collins. 1991. Portfolio documentation and assessment center exercises: A marriage made for teacher assessment. *Teacher Education Quarterly* 18 (3): 13–29.

Vavrus, L., and R. Calfee. 1988. A research strategy for assessing teachers of elementary literacy: The promise of performance portfolios. Paper presented at the annual meeting of the National Reading Conference, Tucson, Arizona.

Wolf, K. 1991. The schoolteacher's portfolio: Practical issues in design implementation and evaluation. *Phi Delta Kappan* (October): 129–36.

Interrater Graduate Portfolio Assessment

STUDENT: _____ ASSESSOR: _____

LEARNING OUTCOME: Communicate Bilingually	EVALUATION	COMMENTS
❖ Can identify linguistic features of ASL and English and discuss specific challenges of these differences for interpreters;	*Direct Evidence* Yes No	
❖ ASL interview—level VIII or greater; monologue and dialogue in ASL demonstrate grammatically correct, register-appropriate ASL;	*Comprehension:* 1 2 3 4 5 minimum superior	
❖ Spoken English sample demonstrates grammatically correct, register-appropriate spoken English.	*Mastery:* 1 2 3 4 5 minimum superior	

Note: *Comprehension:* understands/can explain the content area
    Mastery: degree of demonstrated knowledge/skill and ability to apply to the field of interpreting
    Direct: video, self-authored papers
    Indirect: letters or certificates declaring abilities
    Douglas College©1999. Reprinted by permission.

LEARNING OUTCOME: Act Biculturally	EVALUATION	COMMENTS
❖ Can identify rules for social interaction in both the Deaf and hearing communities;	*Direct Evidence* Yes No	
❖ Can discuss the role of hearing people in the Deaf community and related challenges for interpreters;	*Comprehension:*	
❖ Demonstrates appropriate attention-getting strategies, turn-taking behaviors, and other rules for social interaction in the Deaf community, adapting to a range of contexts and settings as appropriate;	1 2 3 4 5 minimum superior	
❖ Demonstrates appropriate attention-getting strategies, turn-taking behaviors, and other rules for social interaction in the English-speaking community, adapting to a range of contexts and settings as appropriate.	*Mastery:* 1 2 3 4 5 minimum superior	

LEARNING OUTCOME: Act Ethically	EVALUATION	COMMENTS
❖ Demonstrates a pattern of critical thinking when making and discussing professional decisions;	*Direct Evidence* Yes No	
❖ Discusses power, power structures, and systems within which one may work and the implications for interpreters;		
❖ Identifies the underlying principles of the Code of Ethics and relevant laws, applying them to professional decisions;	*Comprehension:* 1 2 3 4 5 minimum superior	
❖ Behaves in ways that support and respect diversity;		
❖ Acts professionally in relationships with consumers, other interpreters, etc. (communicating, problem solving, negotiating, setting boundaries, etc.);	*Mastery:* 1 2 3 4 5 minimum superior	
❖ Participates in professional organizations and upgrading, striving toward national certification.		

LEARNING OUTCOME: Interpret Meaning

	EVALUATION	COMMENTS
❖ Takes in and analyzes linguistic utterances (expressed and implied) and contextual factors to identify essential elements of meaning;	*Direct Evidence* Yes No	
❖ Produces an utterance in the target language that conveys the original meaning/intent and maintains dynamic equivalence between the individuals engaged in the interaction;	*Comprehension:* 1 2 3 4 5 minimum superior	
❖ Monitors work and makes corrections as needed;	*Mastery:* 1 2 3 4 5 minimum superior	
❖ Manages the overall interpreting process (e.g., decides on the use of consecutive or simultaneous interpreting, interrupting the speaker if need be, etc.)		

LEARNING OUTCOME: Take Care of Self

	EVALUATION	COMMENTS
❖ Manages time effectively;	*Direct Evidence* Yes No	
❖ Cares for self emotionally, physically, spiritually, and nutritionally by setting appropriate personal and professional boundaries/goals;	*Comprehension:* 1 2 3 4 5 minimum superior	
❖ Establishes support networks and maintains effective interpersonal communication;	*Mastery:* 1 2 3 4 5 minimum superior	
❖ Reflects on personal practice and sets future goals.		

LEARNING OUTCOME: Use Effective Business Skills

	EVALUATION	COMMENTS
❖ Demonstrates effective interpersonal communications, acting respectfully to all people;	*Direct Evidence* Yes No	
❖ Engages in professional consultations (e.g., with team interpreter, interpreting or Deaf mentor, etc.), including appropriate preparation and debriefing of assignments;	*Comprehension:* 1 2 3 4 5 minimum superior	
❖ Presents a professional demeanor (appropriate attire and deportment) for various settings;		
❖ Follows field standards related to negotiating fees and contracts, self-marketing, invoicing, and accounting;	*Mastery:* 1 2 3 4 5 minimum superior	
❖ Communicates effectively in standard written business English.		

APPENDIX 2

Sample Contract

MEMORANDUM

DATE:

TO: Student C

FROM: Program Coordinator

RE: Incomplete Contract

CC: Dean
       Registrar

I am writing to confirm the discussion you had with your portfolio assessment team on (date). At that time, your team noted that you had successfully mastered four of the six competency areas required for graduation. However, you have not yet mastered (a) communicate bilingually and (b) interpret meaning, which means you have not completed your fourth-semester courses and are not yet ready to graduate.

In order to complete fourth-semester courses with a grade of "mastery," you will be required to:

Re-take the ASL interview and obtain a score of VIII or above;

Re-submit two samples of ASL/English interpretation that are at least 75% successful; include a self-assessment accurately identifying successful and unsuccessful samples of interpretation with explanations of why the identified sections are or are not successful and explaining how to make those sections that are unsuccessful become successful.

These documents must be submitted to the program coordinator no later than Aug. 10, 1999, under the terms of this incomplete extension. In the event this work is not completed, your grade for all fourth-semester courses will convert to "nonmastery," and you will be required to repeat the fourth semester in order to graduate from the interpreting program.

I have read and I agree to the terms of this memorandum.

_____

Student   (Date)

_____

Program Coordinator   (Date)

INDEX

Page numbers in italics indicate tables and figures.

actors: using in interactive role-plays, 93, 106

adjacency pairs, 90–91

Agar, M., 132

American Sign Language: assessing comprehension in, 136–37; direct address in, 146; discourse mapping and, 19–20, 22–56; equivalents for English terms with multiple meanings, *120*; in the history of interpreting, 3–4; issues in English translation, 119; producing texts with discourse mapping, 20–21; student interpreter competencies in, 133–34; teaching literacy skills in, 134; turn-taking signals in, 86

argumentative discourse, x, xi; grammatical features associated with, *xiii–xv*

Arjona, Etilvia, 1, 6

assessment: of equivalence, 22, 47–51; of graduation portfolios, 154, 162; of interpreter training using graduation portfolios, 155, 168; of language comprehension, 136–38

assessment portfolios, 153

attention-getting devices, 88–89

attributing sources, 91

Bakhtin, Mikhail, 9

Bassnett-McGuire, S., 117–18

Bernhardt, E., 137, 139

biculturalism, 7

bilingualism, 7

bottom-up processing, 136

brainstorming, 24–27

"Buying My Condo," 23, 59–60

Callow, Kathleen, x, xi

categorizing, 27

chunking, 44–45

clarification requests, 91–92

codes of ethics, 69, 83

cognitive psychology, 5

cohesive elements, 146

Cokely, D., 109

communicative competence: features of, 137–38

community colleges: history of interpreting programs in, 3–4

competence. *See* language competence

comprehension: assessing, 136–38; in discourse mapping, 19–21, 24–29

concept mapping. *See* discourse mapping

conduit model, 4–8. *See also* neutral model of interpreting

Conference of Interpreter Trainers, 6

Conference on Preparation of Personnel in the Field of Interpreting, ix

consecutive interpreting, 12; discourse mapping applied to, 21–22, 42–46

content: in discourse mapping, 16, 57

context: in discourse mapping, 16, 57; in pragmatics, 113

conversational discourse, x; grammatical features associated with, *xiii–xv*

conversationalization, 80

critical discourse analysis: overview of, 11, 69–70; practice of, 74–80; sample analysis, 78–80; theoretical background, 70–74

cultural untranslatability, 114–15. *See also* equivalence

culture: development of multicultural awareness, 115, 118–20, 129; interpreting and, 68–69; postmodernist notions of, 70–74
curriculum development, 2

Deaf culture, 68
description: in pragmatics, 113
direct address, 146
discourse (*see also* interactive interpreting): Callow's typology, x–xii, *xiii–xv;* critical discourse analysis on, 70, 73–74; definitions of, 132; fundamental aspects of, 16; postmodernist notions of, 73
discourse analysis (*see also* critical discourse analysis): advantages of, 10; discourse mapping and, 11; overview of, 15–16
discourse competence, 138
Discourse Considerations in Translating the Word of God (Callow), x
discourse mapping: applied to comprehending texts, 24–29; applied to consecutive interpreting, 42–46; applied to reconstruction of existing texts, 29–34; applied to simultaneous interpreting, 46–47; applied to translation, 34–42; assessing equivalence and, 22, 47–51; choosing texts for, 18–19, 51–56; goal of, 17, 57; interlingual skills and, 21–22, 34–47; intralingual skills and, 19–21, 23–34; notions of content, context, and form in, 16, 57; overview of, 11, 16–17, 57; sample analysis of example texts, 52–56; sample texts, 22–23, 59–66; spiraling concept in, 21; uses of, 17–18

educators: curriculum development and, 2
English: current state of English studies, 133; issues in American Sign Language translation, 119; terms with multiple meanings, 119, *120;* translating into foreign languages, 117–18; turn-taking signals in, 86
equivalence: assessing, 22, 47–51; problem of, 114–15; as a semiotic category, 119
ethics codes, 69, 83
evaluation. *See* assessment
explanatory discourse, x, xi; grammatical features associated with, *xiii–xv*

Fairclough, Norman, 70, 80
figurative language: translating, 122–23
form. *See* linguistic form
frames/framing, 73, 113

Givon, T., 113, 114
Goffman, Erving, 9
graduation portfolios: assessing, 154, 162; benefits to employers, 167; benefits to students, 166–67; community involvement in, 167; evolution of, 154–55; introducing students to, 158; outcomes criteria, *156–57;* overview of, 12, 153–54; recommendation options, 163; required and optional documentation in, *159–61;* sample assessment form, 170–74; sample case studies, 163–66; sample contract form, *175;* supporting students in, 158, 162; used to evaluate interpreter training programs, 155, 168
grammar: features associated with discourse types, *xiii–xv;* features of competency in, 137–38
greetings, 117–18
Gumperz, John, 9

Habermas, J., 70–71
Halliday, M. A. K., 146
Hatim, B., 48
hortatory discourse, x; grammatical features associated with, *xiii–xv*
Hoza, J., 7–8

idea mapping. *See* discourse mapping
idiomatic language: translating, 122–23
immediate recall protocols: benefits to interpreter training, 139, 149–50; choosing and preparing texts for, 140–41; experiencing the text, 141; introducing to students, 139; overview of, 12; sample class analysis, 143, 145–47; sample individual analysis, 147–49; sample procedure, 142–43; steps in, 139; uses of, 139; using student-generated data, 141–42
instructors: curriculum development and, 2
interactional analysis, 8–10
interactional management strategies, 87–91
interactive interpreting: current notions of,

103, 105, 109–10; early notions of, 6; impact of interpreters' strategies on, 105–6; interactional management strategies for, 87–91; metalinguistic analysis of, 96–97; recognizing and identifying features of, 85–86; relayings in, 91–92; role-plays and, 92–96 (*see also* interactive role-plays); skills development in, 84; using interactive videotapes, 97–98
interactive language processing, 136
interactive role-plays: advance planning for, 98–100; challenges of, 106; choosing participants and topics for, 93–94; effectiveness of, 84, 103; overview of, 11–12; permission form, 95, *96;* post-role-play discussions, 102–3; pre-role-play setup, 100–101; process of, 101–2; scheduling form, *99;* scheduling within courses, 95–96; student analyses of, 103, *104;* teaching objectives for, 85–96; timeliness of concept, 103, 105; videotaping, 95
interactive videotapes, 97–98
interlingual translation, 112; discourse mapping and, 21–22, 34–47
interpreters: introductions and, 87–88; issues of language competency and, 133–35; responses to questions, 90–91
interpreter training: bilingual, bicultural concepts and, 7; codes of ethics and, 69; conferences on, ix, 6; current state of, 1–2; evaluating through graduation portfolios, 155, 168; history and overview of, 3–8; immediate recall protocols and, 139, 149–50; metacognition and, 149; neutral model of interpreting and, 2, 4–8, 68–69; notions of culture and, 68; strategic competence and, 149; student language competencies and, 133–35; task analysis concepts and, 6; using Callow's typology of discourse in, xi–xii; using translation techniques in, 109, 121–29
interpreting/interpretation (*see also* interactive interpreting; translating/translation): cognitive analyses and, 5; definitions of, 15, 110–11; distinguished from translation, 111; equivalency issue and, 114–15; goal of, 112; interactional notions of, 8–10; judgments about people and, 67; neutral model of, 2, 4–8, 68–69, 83–84; pro-

cess of, 128; teaching Deaf culture and, 68; word-based concepts of, 4
intersemiotic translation, 113
intralingual translation, 112; discourse mapping and, 19–21, 23–34
introductions, 87–88

Jakobson, Roman, 112–13
Jefferson, G., 85

languaculture, 132
language acquisition, 134
language competence: features of, 137–38; of student interpreters, 133–35
language comprehension: assessing, 136–38
language-processing models, 135–36
language study: current state of, 132–33
Larson, M. L., 47, 119
lifeworlds, 70–73, *71, 72*
linguistic competence, 137–38
linguistic feature maps, 36–41
linguistic form: in discourse mapping, 16, 57
linguistic signals: recognizing and identifying, 85–86
literacy: concepts of, 132
"Living Fully," 23, 61–66

Malcolm, K., 166
Mason, I., 48
meaning(s): multiple, problems for translation, 117–20; in pragmatics, 113; processing, models of, 135–36
medical exams, 7–8
metacognition: described, 135; models of language processing, 135–36; significance to interpreter training, 149
metalinguistic analyses, 96–97
metaphors: translating, 126
Metzger, M., 8–9
mind mapping. *See* discourse mapping
multicultural awareness, 115, 118–20, 129
multiple meanings, 117–20

"Name Change," 141
narrative discourse, x–xi
Neubert, A., 119
neutral model of interpreting, 2, 4–8; criticisms of, 68–69, 83–84; Registry of

neutral model of interpreting (*continued*)
Interpreters for the Deaf Code of Ethics
and, 83
Nida, E. A., 47, 115

Oller, J. W., Jr., 15, 113
overlaps: managing interactively, 89–90

point of view: in pragmatics, 113
portfolios, 153. *See also* graduation portfolios
postmodernism: critical discourse analysis
and, 70; notions of culture and discourse
in, 70–74
pragmatics, 113
procedural discourse, x–xi; grammatical
features associated with, *xiii–xv*; professionals: using in interactive role-plays,
93, 94, 106
pronominal references, 92, 146
public sphere, 70–71, *71*, *72*

question-answer sequences, 90–91

recall protocols. *See* immediate recall
protocols
Reddy, M., 6, 134
Regional Interpreter Training Consortium,
122, 123, 126
Registry of Interpreters for the Deaf (RID),
ix, 83
relayings, 91–92
remedial instruction, 134
reported speech, 146
rhemes, 146
RID. *See* Registry of Interpreters for the
Deaf
role-playing. *See* interactive role-plays
Roy, Cynthia, xii, 6, 8, 109

Sacks, H., 85
Saussure, Ferdinand de, 114
Schegloff, E., 85
second language study: current state of,
132–33
Seleskovitch, D., 115–16, 128
"Semantic Awareness Assessment," 125
semiotic category concept, 119
semiotics, 112

semiotic transformation, 112, 113–14
sequential maps: in consecutive interpreting, 43; in the retelling of texts, 31–33; in
translation, 36–41
simultaneous interpreting, 12; discourse
mapping and, 46–47; in the history of
interpreting training, 4
sociolinguistic competence, 138
source attribution, 91
statements. *See* discourse
Stokoe, William, ix
strategic competence, 149
Street, Brian, 71, 73
student evaluation. *See* graduation portfolios
student interpreters: issues of language
competency and, 133–35
summonses, 88–89
surface structures, 112

Taber, C., 115
task analysis, 6
text-forming devices, 146
texts: choosing and preparing for immediate
recall protocols, 140–41; choosing for
critical discourse analysis, 74; choosing
for discourse mapping, 18–19, 51–56;
choosing for translation techniques, 121–
23; comprehending with discourse mapping, 19–21, 24–29; producing with discourse mapping, 19–21; reconstructing
in discourse mapping, 29–34
themes, 146
top-down processing, 135
translating/translation (*see also* interpret-
ing/interpretation): chunking, 44–45;
definitions of, 110–11; development of
multilingual/multicultural awareness in,
115, 118–20, 129; discourse mapping
applied to, 21, 34–42; distinguished from
interpretation, 111; equivalency issue
and, 114–15; goal of, 112; multiple
meanings of words and, 117–20; restructuring messages and discarding source
words, 115–16; theoretical basis, 112–14;
types of, 112–13
translation techniques: choosing texts for,
121–23; classroom activity in, 124–25;
incorporating in interpreter training, 121;
preparing model translations, 123; sample

texts, 125–27; teaching and learning outcomes, 127–29; theoretical basis of, 111–14; usefulness to interpreter training, 109

anslation theory, 112–14, 129

.rn-taking, 85–86; managing interactively, 89–90

niversities: history of interpreting programs in, 3–4

'an Lier, L., 133

ideo cameras, 95

videotapes: interactive, 97–98
videotaping: of interactive role-plays, 95
vox pops, 76, 79–80

Wadensjö, C., 8, 9
Wodak, Ruth, 73
words: discarding during translation/interpretation, 115–16; multiple meanings and, 117–20

Zimmer, J., 84